funky
chunky
crocheted accessories

60 ways and more to make and customize hats,
bags, scarves, mittens and slippers

jan eaton

David and Charles

A DAVID & CHARLES BOOK

David & Charles is an F+W Publications
Inc. company
4700 East Galbraith Road
Cincinnati, OH 45236

First UK edition published 2006

Conceived and produced by
Breslich & Foss Ltd, London

Volume © Breslich & Foss Ltd, 2006
Text: **Jan Eaton**
Photography: **Martin Norris**
Design: **Elizabeth Healey**
Project Management: **Janet Ravenscroft**

A catalogue record for this book is available
from the British Library.

ISBN-13: 978-0-7153-2435-6
ISBN-10: 0-7153-2435-7

Printed in China
for David & Charles
Brunel House   Newton Abbot   Devon

Visit our website at
www.davidandcharles.co.uk

David & Charles books are available from
all good bookshops; alternatively you can
contact our Orderline on 0870 9908222 or
write to us at FREEPOST EX2 110, D&C
Direct, Newton Abbot, TQ12 4ZZ (no
stamp required UK only).

contents

introduction

In this book, you will discover how to turn five easy-to-make crochet patterns into over 60 delightfully individual accessories. By combining edgings, fastenings, and a wide range of embellishments with chunky crochet, you can make items that are truly unique.

Begin by checking out the Basic Techniques section on pages 8 to 23. Here you'll find all the information you need to take up the craft of crochet and become accustomed to choosing yarn and working with a crochet hook. Each technique is presented in an easy-to-understand sequence of instructions illustrated with close-up photographs that will encourage you every step of the way.

Once you've become familiar with basic crochet skills, it's time to move on and begin working the basic patterns on pages 24 to 29. Whether you want to crochet a scarf, bag, hat, pair of slippers, or mittens, you'll find these basic accessories are simple to make. If you're a newcomer to the craft of crochet but can handle making a foundation chain and working the basic stitches, you're ready to make your first scarf. As your skills and confidence improve with practice, try the bag and hat. When you are more proficient, make the slippers and mittens.

When you have mastered the basics, turn to the next chapters and discover how to adapt accessories so they truly suit your style. Drawing on a wealth of decorative ideas and suggestions, there are over 60 inspiring accessories based around the five basic patterns. To make it easy to find your way around the book, the designs are divided into three sections. Edgings and Trimmings (pages 30 to 53), shows you how to craft different types of edgings and trimmings including fringes, ruffles, edging variations, pockets, flower trims, and tassels. Fastenings and Handles (pages 54 to 75), shows you how to make and attach different styles of handles and fastenings including grab handles, crochet buttons, earflaps, braids, sporty tabs, and toggle fastenings. Beading and Embellishing (pages 76 to 97), adds sparkle and glitz with beads, jewels, bells, and charms. We show you how to crochet beads into your work, and how to decorate crochet fabric with embellishments.

The final chapter, Customizing Crochet (pages 98 to 117) contains inspiring suggestions and helpful hints for exploring the boundaries of crochet to make something different. This chapter shows you how to improvise your own variations of the basic patterns, how to add stripes and different stitch patterns to your accessories, and how to work with novelty yarns. It also covers easy washing-machine felting, working surface crochet, and using recycled materials.

At the back of the book, starting on page 118, you'll find the illustrated Gallery which contains a photograph of every accessory and variation in the book. The designs are arranged by subject so that accessories of all the same type are shown together. We hope you will be inspired by our designs to customize the basic accessories to fit your own unique style.

jan eaton

chapter 1
basic techniques and patterns

This introductory section contains everything you need to know to get started in the craft of crochet and make your own **personalized accessories**. From **choosing** and handling yarns and crochet hooks to **blocking** finished pieces, and from **joining** a new yarn to making up the accessories, all the essentials are shown here in clear step-by-step photographs. Once you have mastered the art of working crochet stitches, turn to the **Basic Patterns on page 24**. Here you'll find instructions for making the Scarf, Buttonhole Bag, Hat, Slippers and Mittens.

Materials

A crochet hook, a ball of chunky yarn and a basic sewing kit are all you need to get started with this fascinating craft. Yarn and hooks come in a range of different weights, materials and sizes and the information in this section will help you choose which to buy.

YARN

All the projects in this book can be made with your own choice of yarn colours and fibre composition. Many crocheters prefer pure wool yarns, but there are times when synthetic yarns may be preferable, such as for items that require frequent washing. Wool yarns may be more expensive than wool/synthetic blends and those made entirely from synthetics. You may prefer to use a pure cotton or synthetic/cotton blend yarn as these are less itchy than some made from wool.

Be adventurous and incorporate textured yarns, such as eyelash, tweed, or ribbon yarn in your accessory, but try to combine yarns of similar weight. As well as chunky weight yarns, you can use finer weights and crochet with two or more strands held together to make a thicker yarn. To make up a chunky yarn weight, try combining the following:

Each sample: one strand of chunky yarn

Left to right: One strand of Aran yarn plus one strand 4ply; three strands of 4ply; two samples of two strands of double knitting

Left to right: Two strands of ribbon; one strand of plain double knitting, one strand of space-dyed double knitting; one strand of Aran, one strand of ribbon; one strand of double knitting, one strand of novelty yarn

HOOKS

Crochet hooks are made from aluminium, wood, bamboo, plastic or resin and come in a range of sizes from small (2.25mm/US size B) to large (19mm/US size S) to suit different weights of yarn. Smaller steel hooks are used to work very fine crochet in cotton thread. Choose whichever type of hook is comfortable to use.

Useful yarn/hook combinations

4ply (Sport weight)
2.25–3.5mm (US sizes B–E)

Double knitting (DK)
3.75 and 4.5mm (US sizes F and G)

Aran (Worsted weight)
5mm and 5.5mm (US sizes H and I)

Chunky (Chunky weight)
5.5–8mm (US sizes I–L)

CROCHET EQUIPMENT
Yarn needles

Sewing needles with blunt tips and large eyes are available in a range of sizes to suit different yarn weights. Yarn needles may be straight or have bent tips.

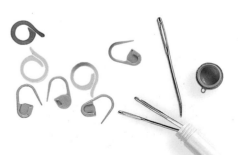

Row counter

A row counter is useful for keeping track of the number of rows you work.

Split ring stitch markers

Slip one of these onto your crochet to mark your place. Slip markers into a foundation chain at regular intervals to help you keep an accurate count.

Tape measure

Fibreglass tapes are best as they do not stretch. Buy one that has both imperial and metric measurements.

Scissors

Buy a small pair with sharp points. If you keep scissors in your work bag, buy a pair with a sheath.

Pins

Glass or plastic-headed pins are easy to see and don't slip through crocheted fabric. Also available are extra long marking pins.

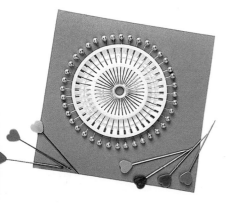

Holding the hook and yarn

There is no right or wrong way to hold the yarn and hook when you are crocheting: experiment until you find the most comfortable method. Hold the hook like a pen or overhand like a knife in your right hand and control the yarn with your left hand by feeding it through and around your fingers. (If you are left handed, simply reverse the information in this section.)

HOLDING THE HOOK

1 The most common way to handle a hook is to hold it like a pen. Centre the tips of your right thumb and forefinger over the flat section of the hook.

2 Another way to hold the hook is to grasp the flat section between your right thumb and forefinger as if you were holding a knife.

HOLDING THE YARN

To control the yarn supply, loop the short end of the yarn over your left forefinger and take the yarn coming from the ball loosely around the ring finger on the same hand to tension it. Use your middle finger to help hold the work as you crochet. If it feels more comfortable, tension the yarn around your little finger instead.

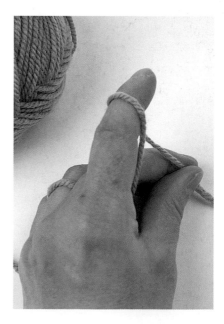

Starting to crochet

The first step when starting to crochet is to make a chain of the number of stitches given in the pattern, beginning with a slip knot. This is called the foundation chain and the first row of stitches is worked into it. There are different ways of inserting the hook into the chains and each produces a different kind of edge.

front   back

MAKING A SLIP KNOT

All types of crochet begin by making a slip knot to anchor the end of the yarn. Make the knot with your fingers, then slip it onto the hook.

1 With about 15cm (6in) of the end of the yarn on the left, loop the yarn around your right forefinger. Carefully slip the loop off your finger. Holding the loop in your right hand, push a loop of the short end of the yarn through the first loop.

2 Insert the hook into the second loop. Gently pull the short end of the yarn to tighten the loop around the hook and complete the slip knot.

WORKING THE FOUNDATION CHAIN

The foundation chain is the crochet equivalent of casting on in knitting and it's important to make the required number of chains for the pattern you are going to follow.

1 Holding the hook with the slip knot in your right hand and the yarn in your left, wrap the yarn over the hook. This is known as 'yarn over' or 'yarn over hook' and you should always wrap the yarn over the hook this way.

2 Draw the yarn through to make a new loop and complete the first stitch of the chain.

3 Repeat this step, drawing a new loop of yarn through the loop on the hook until the chain is the required length. Move up the thumb and finger of the hand that is grasping the chain after every few stitches to keep tension even.

COUNTING CHAINS

The front of the chain looks like a series of V shapes or little hearts, while the back of the chain forms a distinctive 'bump' of yarn behind each V shape. Count the stitches on either the front or back of the chain (whichever you find easier), counting each chain as one stitch, except for the chain on the hook, which is not counted.

1

2

2

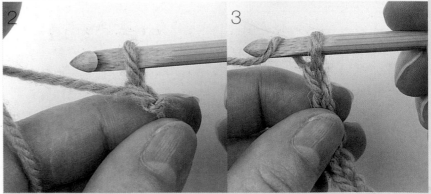

3

1

WORKING INTO THE FOUNDATION CHAIN

You're now ready to work the first row of stitches into the chain. The hook can be inserted into different places on the chain, but this is the easiest method for the beginner to use, although it results in a rather loose edge.

1 Holding the chain with the front facing you, insert the hook into the top loop of the chain and work the first stitch as stated in the pattern.

2 To make a stronger, neater edge, turn the chain so the back of it is facing you. Work the first row of stitches as instructed in the pattern, inserting the hook through the 'bump' at the back of each chain stitch.

Tip

If you find it difficult to work the first row of stitches into the foundation chain because the chains are too tight, try using a hook one size larger to work the chain. Switch to the hook size suggested in the pattern after you've worked the chain.

TURNING CHAINS

When working crochet in rows or rounds, you will need to work a specific number of extra chains at the beginning of each row or round. The extra chains are needed to bring the hook up to the correct height for the particular stitch you will work next. When the work is turned at the end of a straight row, these extra chains are called a 'turning chain', and when they are worked at the beginning of a round, they are called a 'starting chain'.

The list in the box (right) shows the correct number of chain stitches needed to make a turn for each type of stitch. If you are inclined to work chain stitches very tightly, you may find that you need to work an extra chain in order to prevent the edges of your work from becoming too tight.

Double crochet stitch:
1 turning chain

Half treble crochet stitch:
2 turning chains

Treble crochet stitch:
3 turning chains

The turning or starting chain is usually counted as the first stitch of the row, except when working double crochet where the single turning chain is ignored. For example, 'ch 3 (counts as 1 tr)' at the beginning of a row or round means that the turning or starting chain contains three chain stitches and these are counted as the equivalent of one treble crochet stitch. A turning or starting chain may be longer than the number required for the stitch and in that case, counts as one stitch plus a number of chains. For example, 'ch 5 (counts as 1 tr, ch 2)' means that the turning or starting chain is the equivalent of one treble crochet stitch plus two chain stitches.

At the end of the row or round, the final stitch is usually worked into the turning or starting chain worked on the previous row or round. The final stitch may be worked into the top chain of the turning or starting chain or into another specified stitch of the chain. For example, '1 tr into 3rd of ch-3' means that the final stitch is a treble crochet stitch and it is worked into the third stitch of the turning or starting chain.

WORKING A SLIP STITCH

Slip stitch is rarely used to create a crochet fabric on its own. Instead, it is used to join rounds of crochet and to move the hook and yarn across a group of existing stitches to a new position.

1 To work a slip stitch into the foundation chain, insert the hook from front to back under the top loop of the second chain from the hook.

2 Wrap the yarn over the hook and draw it through both the chain and the loop on the hook. One loop remains on the hook and 1 slip stitch has been worked.

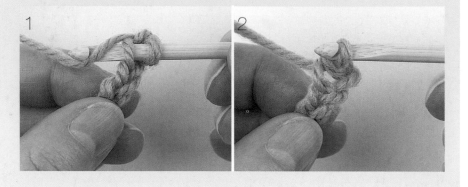

WORKING A DOUBLE CROCHET STITCH

Double crochet is the shortest crochet stitch and it makes a firm, sturdy fabric with a dense texture. It needs pressing or blocking well (page 22) as the fabric has a tendency to curl upwards at the edges.

1 Work the foundation chain and insert the hook from front to back under the top loop of the second chain from the hook. Wrap the yarn over the hook and draw it through the first loop, leaving 2 loops on the hook.

2 To complete the stitch, wrap the yarn over the hook and draw it through both loops on the hook. Continue in this way along the row, working 1 double crochet stitch into each chain.

3 At the end of the row, work 1 chain for a turning chain (remember this chain does not count as a stitch) and turn the work.

4 Insert the hook from front to back under both loops of the first double crochet stitch at the beginning of the row. Work a double crochet stitch into each stitch of the previous row.

5 Work the final double crochet stitch into the last stitch of the row below, but not into the turning chain.

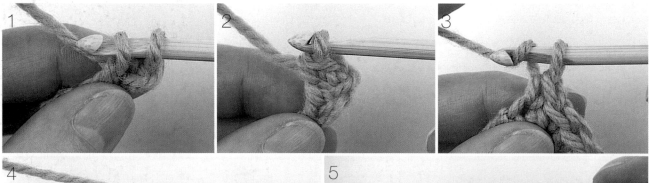

WORKING A HALF TREBLE CROCHET STITCH

Halfway in height between double and treble crochet, half treble crochet makes a firm fabric with slightly more elasticity than double crochet. The fabric has horizontal ridges on both front and back.

1 Wrap the yarn over the hook before inserting it into the work.

2 Insert the hook from front to back into the work. (If you are at the beginning of the foundation chain, insert the hook under the top loop of the third chain from the hook.)

3 Draw the yarn through the chain, leaving 3 loops on the hook.

4 Wrap the yarn over the hook and draw it through all 3 loops on the hook. One loop remains on the hook and 1 half treble crochet stitch has been worked.

5 Continue along the row, working 1 half treble crochet stitch into each chain. At the end of the row, work 2 chains for the turning chain and turn the work.

6 Skipping the first half treble crochet stitch at the beginning of the row, wrap the yarn over the hook, insert the hook from front to back under both loops of the second stitch on the previous row, and work a half treble crochet stitch into each stitch made on the previous row.

7 At the end of the row, work the last stitch into the top stitch of the turning chain.

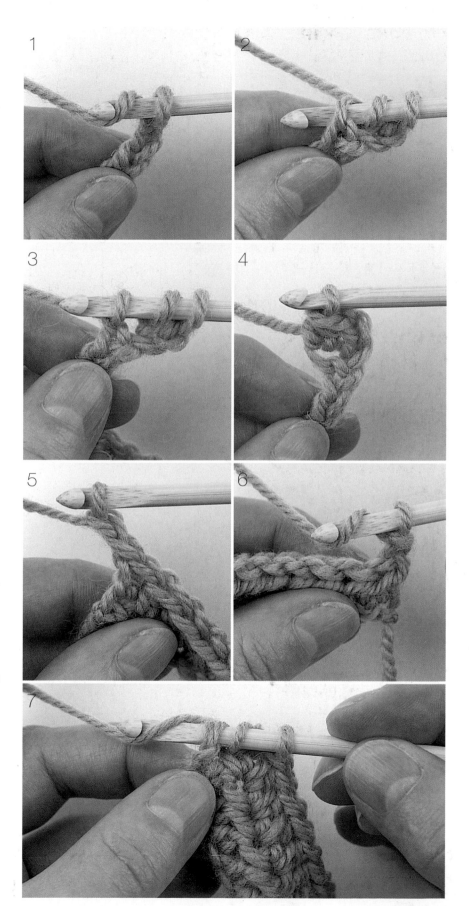

WORKING A TREBLE CROCHET STITCH

Taller than either of the previous two stitches, treble crochet is easy to work and the fabric grows quickly. It has a more open appearance than double crochet and less tendency to curl up at the edges.

1 Wrap the yarn over the hook and insert the hook from front to back into the work. (If you are at the beginning of the foundation chain, insert the hook under the top loop of the fourth chain from the hook.) Draw the yarn through the chain, leaving 3 loops on the hook.

2 Wrap the yarn over the hook and draw it through the first 2 loops on the hook. Two loops remain on the hook.

3 Wrap the yarn over the hook. Draw the yarn through the 2 loops on the hook. One loop remains on the hook and 1 treble crochet stitch has been worked.

4 At the end of the row, work 3 chains for the turning chain and turn the work.

5 Skipping the first treble crochet stitch at the beginning of the row, wrap the yarn over the hook, insert the hook from front to back under both loops of the second stitch on the previous row, and work a treble crochet stitch into each stitch made on the previous row.

6 At the end of the row, work the last stitch into the top stitch of the turning chain.

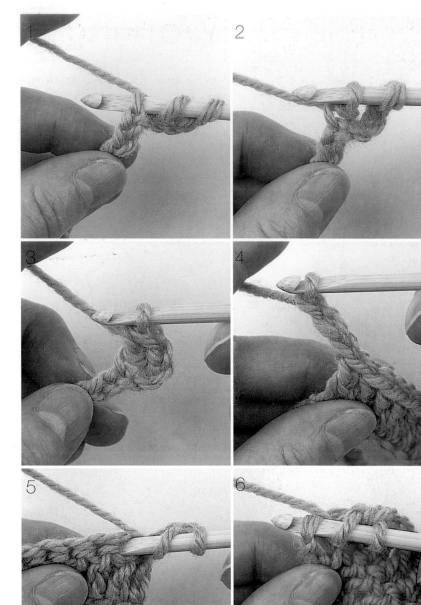

WORKING INTO THE BACK LOOP

Unless specific pattern instructions tell you otherwise, it's usual to work most crochet stitches by taking the hook under both loops of the stitches made on the previous row. By working under the back loop of a stitch, the unworked loop becomes a horizontal bar that creates ridged fabric.

   To work into the back of a row of stitches, insert the hook under the back loops of the stitches on the previous row.

single crochet

half double crochet

double crochet

Working in rounds

Crochet can easily be worked in rounds, beginning at the centre and working outwards. To make the foundation, work a short length of chain and join it into a ring.

1 Begin making the foundation ring by working a short length of chain (page 14). Work the number of chains stated in the pattern and join into a ring by working a slip stitch (page 16) into the first stitch of the foundation chain. Gently tighten the first stitch by pulling the loose yarn end with your left hand. The foundation ring is now complete.

2 Work the number of starting chains stated in the pattern: 3 chains are shown here and will count as a treble crochet stitch.

3 Inserting the hook into the space at the centre of the ring each time, work the correct number of stitches into the ring as stated in the pattern. Count the stitches at the end of the round to make sure you have worked the correct number.

4 Join the first and last stitches of the round together by working a slip stitch into the top of the starting chain.

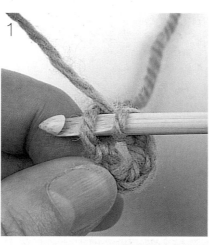

Joining a new yarn

Always join new yarn at the side of the work, not in the middle of a row, to help prevent the yarn ends unravelling and making a hole in your work. Join the new yarn as you work the last stitch of the row, whether working in double or treble crochet.

JOINING A NEW YARN IN DOUBLE CROCHET

1 Join the new colour at the end of the last row worked in the previous colour. To work the last stitch, draw a loop of the old yarn through so there are 2 loops on the hook and loop the new yarn around the hook.

2 Pull the new yarn through both stitches on the hook. Turn and work the next row with the new colour.

JOINING A NEW YARN IN TREBLE CROCHET

1 Join the new colour at the end of the last row worked in the previous colour. Leaving the last stage of the final stitch incomplete, loop the new yarn around the hook and pull it though the stitches on the hook to complete the stitch.

2 Turn and work the next row with the new colour. Knot the 2 loose ends together before cutting off the excess yarn, leaving a tail of about 10cm (4in). Always undo the knot before darning in the yarn ends.

FASTENING OFF YARN

To fasten off the yarn at the end of a piece of crochet, cut the yarn 15cm (6in) from the last stitch and pull the yarn end through the stitch with the hook. (Right.)

DEALING WITH YARN ENDS

Thread the end of the yarn in a yarn needle. Darn the end through several stitches on the wrong side of the work. Trim the remaining yarn. (Far right.)

OVERCAST SEAM

Crochet pieces are easy to join together as the edges are very stable. Use the same yarn for seaming as for your project and take care to fasten off the yarn ends securely.

1 Pin the crochet pieces together with right sides facing, inserting the pins vertically a few stitches away from the edge. Secure the yarn by taking a few stitches over the top of the edge.

2 With your index finger between the layers, insert the needle from back to front through both layers as close to the edge as you can. Repeat evenly along the seam.

MAKING A BUTTONHOLE

Working a two-row horizontal buttonhole is the neatest method of making any size of buttonhole and has the advantage of not needing any reinforcing. You can make this type of buttonhole on either a right side row as shown, or on a wrong side row.

1 On a right side row, work in double crochet to the position of the buttonhole, skip the number of stitches indicated in the pattern, and work the same number of chains over the skipped stitches.

2 Anchor the chain by working a double crochet stitch after the skipped stitches. Continue along the row working single crochet stitches.

3 On the return (wrong side) row, work a double crochet stitch into each stitch. When you reach the buttonhole, work a double crochet stitch into each chain, then complete the row in double crochet.

Shaping crochet

There are several different ways to shape crochet by increasing or decreasing the number of working stitches. Adding or subtracting one or two stitches at intervals along a row of crochet is the easiest way and the methods shown on this page can be used with double, half treble and double crochet stitches.

DECREASING

To decrease one stitch along a row of crochet, either skip one stitch or work two adjacent stitches together. To decrease two stitches, work three adjacent stitches together to make one stitch. The easiest way to decrease one stitch – whether working in double or treble crochet – is by simply skipping the next stitch of the row, as shown below.

INCREASING

1 The simplest method of adding a double stitch to a row of double crochet is by working 2 double crochet stitches into 1 stitch on the previous row.

2 This type of increase is also used when working treble crochet. Work 2 treble crochet stitches into 1 stitch on the previous row.

WORKING TWO OR THREE STITCHES TOGETHER

1 Decrease 1 double crochet stitch by working 2 stitches together (known as 'dc2tog'). Leave the first stitch incomplete so there are 2 loops on the hook.

2 Draw the yarn through the next stitch so there are 3 loops on the hook.

3 To finish the decrease, wrap the yarn over and pull through all 3 loops on the hook.

4 Two stitches can be decreased in the same way by working 3 double crochet stitches together (known as 'dc3tog').

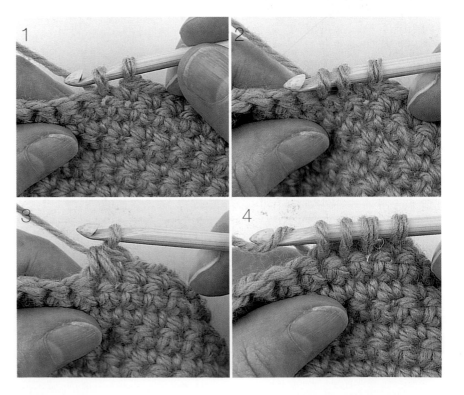

Tension

The term 'tension' refers to the number of stitches and rows contained in a given width and length of crocheted fabric. The patterns in this book include a recommended tension for the yarn used and it's important that you match this tension so your work comes out the right size. This is usually quoted as 'x stitches and y rows to 10cm (4in)' measured over a certain stitch pattern using a certain size of hook. Tension can be affected by the type of yarn, the size and brand of the hook, and the type of stitch pattern. For some items, such as scarves and bags, getting the correct tension is less important than when making mittens or slippers, where a good fit is crucial.

MAKING AND MEASURING A TENSION SAMPLE

Read the pattern instructions to find the recommended tension. Working in the exact yarn you will use for the item, make a sample 15–20cm (6–8 in) wide. Work in the required stitch until the piece is 15–20cm (6–8 in) long. Fasten off the yarn. Block the tension sample using the method suited to the yarn fibre content and allow to dry.

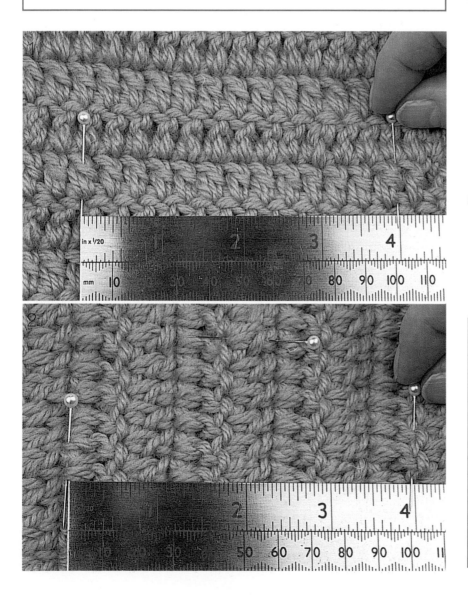

1 Lay the sample right side up on a flat surface and use a ruler or tape measure to measure 10cm (4in) horizontally across a row of stitches. Mark this measurement by inserting 2 pins exactly 10cm (4in) apart. Make a note of the number of stitches (including partial stitches) between the pins. This is the number of stitches to 10cm (4in).

2 Turn the sample on its side. Working in the same way, measure 10cm (4in) across the rows, again inserting 2 pins exactly 10cm (4in) apart. Make a note of the number of rows (including partial rows) between the pins. This is the number of rows to 10cm (4in).

Ball bands

The ball band – or paper tag on yarn – has lots of useful information printed on it, including the fibre content of the yarn, its weight and the yardage of the ball or skein. Some bands also include suggested crochet hook sizes and gauge measurements, as well as washing or dry-cleaning information.

HOW TO ADJUST THE TENSION

If you have too many stitches or rows between the pins inserted in your tension sample, your tension is too tight and you should make another sample using a hook one size larger. If you have too few stitches or rows between the pins, your tension is too loose and you should make another sample using a hook one size smaller. Block the new sample and measure the tension as before. Repeat this process until your tension matches that given in the pattern.

PRESSING CROCHETED FABRIC

Press the fabric lightly on the wrong side, setting your iron temperature according to the information given on the ball band of your yarn. Avoid pressing synthetic yarns as they will become limp and lifeless – or melt – with too much heat.

BLOCKING CROCHETED FABRIC

Blocking involves pinning a piece of crocheted fabric to the correct size, then either steaming it with an iron or moistening with cold water depending on the fibre content of the yarn. Pin your finished item to the correct size on a flat surface, such as an ironing board or a specialist blocking board, using rust-proof pins. It is a good idea to block gauge samples (page 21) before measuring them.

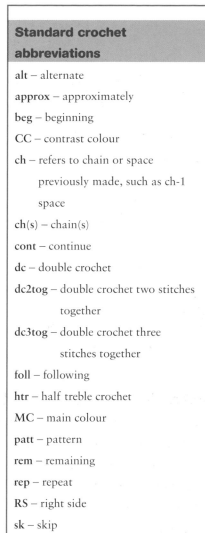

Standard crochet abbreviations

alt – alternate

approx – approximately

beg – beginning

CC – contrast colour

ch – refers to chain or space previously made, such as ch-1 space

ch(s) – chain(s)

cont – continue

dc – double crochet

dc2tog – double crochet two stitches together

dc3tog – double crochet three stitches together

foll – following

htr – half treble crochet

MC – main colour

patt – pattern

rem – remaining

rep – repeat

RS – right side

sk – skip

sl st – slip stitch

sp(s) – space(s)

st(s) – stitch(es)

tr – treble crochet

WS – wrong side

Woollens

(Above) To block woollen yarns with warm steam, hold a steam iron set at the correct temperature for the yarn about 2cm (^{3}/4in) above the surface of the crochet and let the steam penetrate for several seconds without allowing the iron to come into contact with the fabric. Lay the board flat and allow to dry before removing the pins.

Synthetics

(Below) To block synthetic and wool/synthetic blend yarns, pin out as above, then use a spray bottle to mist the item with clean cold water until it is evenly moist all over, but not saturated. Pat with your hand to help the moisture penetrate more easily. Lay the board flat and allow to dry before removing the pins.

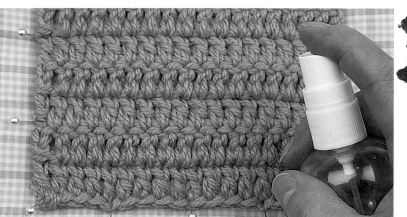

Basic Patterns

This section of the book contains basic patterns for a crocheted scarf, buttonhole bag, hat and pairs of slippers and mittens. If you're a beginner, start by making the basic scarf on this page, then try the hat on page 26.

THE BASIC SCARF

YOU WILL NEED

- 2 balls of pure wool chunky yarn with approx 92m (100yd) per 100g ball
- 6mm (size J) and 6.5mm (size K) crochet hooks or sizes needed to achieve tension
- Yarn needle

FINISHED SIZE

Scarf measures 15cm (6in) wide and 102cm (6in) long.

TENSION

12 stitches and 6 rows to 10cm (4in) measured over treble crochet, using 6mm (size J) crochet hook.

CROCHETING THE SCARF

Using 6.5mm (size K) hook, work 22ch.

Change to 6mm (size J) hook.

ROW 1: ((RS) 1tr into 4th ch from hook, 1tr into each ch to end, turn.

ROW 2: 3ch (counts as 1tr), 1tr into each tr of previous row, working last tr into 3rd of beg missed 3ch, turn.

ROW 3: 3ch (counts as 1 tr), 1tr into each tr of previous row, working last tr into 3rd of 3ch, turn.

Rep Row 3 until scarf measures 102cm (40in) long, ending with a RS row.

Fasten off yarn.

FINISHING THE SCARF

Press lightly on the wrong side (Pressing, page 22). Darn the yarn ends on the wrong side using the yarn needle (Dealing With Yarn Ends, page 18).

THE BASIC BAG – BUTTONHOLE BAG

YOU WILL NEED

- 2 balls of pure wool chunky yarn with approx 92m (100yds) per 100g ball
- 6mm (size J) and 6.5mm (size K) crochet hooks or sizes needed to achieve tension
- Yarn needle

FINISHED SIZE

Bag measures 24cm (9½in) wide and 28cm (11in) long.

TENSION

14 stitches and 16 rows to 10cm (4in) measured over double crochet, using 6mm (size J) crochet hook.

CROCHETING THE BAG FRONT

Using 6.5mm (size K) hook; work 33ch.

Change to 6mm (size J) hook.

ROW 1: (RS) 1 dc into 2nd ch from hook, 1 dc into each ch to end, turn.

ROW 2: 1ch, 1dc into each dc of previous row, turn. (32 dc)

Rep Row 2 twenty-seven times more, ending with a RS row.

Make buttonhole

ROW 1: (WS) 1ch, 1dc into each of next 10dc, 12ch, miss next 12dc, 1dc into each of next 10dc, turn.

ROW 2: 1ch, 1dc into each of next 10dc, 1dc into each of next 12ch, 1dc into each of next 10dc, turn. (32dc)

Make handle

ROW 1: 1ch, 1dc into each dc of previous row, turn.

Rep Row 1 three times more, ending with a RS row.

Fasten off yarn.

CROCHETING THE BAG BACK

Work as for front.

FINISHING THE BAG

Press the pieces lightly on the wrong side (Pressing, page 22). Darn the yarn ends on the wrong side using the yarn needle (Dealing With Yarn Ends, page 18). Place the pieces together with right sides facing and pin around the edges. Using the same yarn in the yarn needle, join side and base seams. Turn bag to right side.

THE BASIC HAT

YOU WILL NEED

- 1 ball of pure wool chunky yarn with approx 92m (100yds) per 100g ball
- 6mm (size J) crochet hook or size needed to achieve tension
- Yarn needle

FINISHED SIZE

Hat measures 8 in. (20 cm) deep and 22 in. (56 cm) in circumference and will fit average adult head.

TENSION

12 stitches and 6½ rows to 10cm (4in) measured over treble crochet.

MAKING THE HAT

FOUNDATION RING: Work 6ch and join with ss to form a ring.

ROUND 1: 3ch (counts as 1tr), 15tr into ring, join with ss into 3rd of 3ch. (16tr)

ROUND 2. 3ch (counts as 1tr), 1tr into same stitch, 2tr into each rem tr of previous round, join with ss into 3rd of 3ch. (32tr)

ROUND 3: 3ch (counts as 1tr), 1tr into same stitch, * 1tr into each of next 3tr, 2tr into next tr; rep from * to last 3tr, 1tr into each of next 3tr, join with ss into 3rd of 3ch. (40tr)

ROUND 4: 3ch (counts as 1tr), 1tr into same stitch, * 1tr into each of next 4tr, 2tr into next tr; rep from * to last 4tr, 1tr into each of next 4tr, join with ss into 3rd of 3ch. (48tr)

ROUND 5: 3ch (counts as 1tr), 1tr into same stitch, * 1tr into each of next 5tr, 2tr into next tr; rep from * to last 5tr, 1tr into each of next 5tr, join with ss into 3rd of 3ch. (56tr)

ROUND 6: 3ch (counts as 1tr), 1tr into same stitch, * 1tr into each of next 6tr, 2tr into next tr; rep from * to last 6tr, 1tr into each of next 6tr, join with ss into 3rd of 3ch. (64tr)

ROUNDS 7–10: 3ch (counts as 1tr), miss first tr, 1tr into each rem tr of previous round, join with ss into 3rd of 3ch.

ROUND 11: 1ch, 1dc into same stitch, 1dc into each rem tr of previous round, join with ss into first dc.

ROUNDS 12–14: 1ch, 1dc into same stitch, 1dc into each rem dc of previous round, join with ss into first dc.
Fasten off yarn.

FINISHING THE HAT

Press lightly on the wrong side (Pressing, page 22). Darn the yarn ends on the wrong side using the yarn needle (Dealing With Yarn Ends, page 18).

THE BASIC SLIPPERS

YOU WILL NEED

- 2 [2, 3] balls of pure wool Icelandic Lopi yarn with approx 100m (109yds) per 100g ball
- 6mm (size J) and 6.5mm (size K) crochet hooks or sizes needed to achieve tension
- Yarn needle

FINISHED SIZE

To fit sizes Small (to fit up to 23cm/9in sole), Medium (to fit up to 25.5cm/10in sole) and Large (to fit up to 28cm/11in sole). Instructions for Medium and Large sizes are given in square brackets.

TENSION

14 stitches and 16 rows to 10cm (4in) measured over double crochet worked with 6mm (size J) hook.

MAKING THE SLIPPERS (make two)

FOUNDATION CHAIN: Using 6.5mm (size K) hook, work 21 [25, 29] ch.

Change to 6mm (size J) hook.

ROUND 1: (RS) 2dc into 2nd ch from hook, 1dc into each of next 9 [11, 13] ch, 1htr into next ch, 1tr into each of next 7 [9, 11] ch; 2tr into next ch, 4tr into last ch; working along opposite side of chain, 2tr into next ch, 1tr into each of next 7 [9, 11] ch, 1htr into next ch, 1dc into each of next 9 [11, 13] ch, 2dc into last ch, join with ss into first dc. (47 [55, 63] sts)

ROUND 2: 1ch, 1dc into first st, 2dc into next st, 1dc into each of next 12 [14, 16] sts, 1htr into each of next 8 [10, 12] sts, 2htr into next st, 3htr into next st, 2htr into next st, 1htr into each of next 8 [10, 12] sts, 1dc into each of next 13 [15, 17] sts, 2dc into last st, join with ss into first dc. (53 [61, 69] sts)

ROUND 3: 1ch, 1dc into first st, 2dc into next st, 1dc into each of next 10 [12, 14] sts, miss next st, 1dc into each of next 11 [13, 15] sts, 2dc into next st, 1dc into each of next 5 sts, 2dc into next st, 1dc into each of next 11 [13, 15] sts, miss next st, 1dc into each of next 9 [11, 13] sts, 2dc into last st, join with ss into first dc. (55 [63, 71] sts)

ROUNDS 4, 5 and 6: 1ch, 1dc into each st of previous round, join with ss into first dc.

ROUND 7: 1ch, 1dc into each of next 20 [24, 28] sts, [dc2tog, 1dc into next st] three times, [1dc into next st, dc2tog] three times, 1dc into each of next 17 [21, 25] sts, join with ss into first dc. (49 [57, 65] sts)

ROUND 8: 1ch, 1dc into each of next 20 [24, 28] sts, dc2tog six times, 1dc into each of next 17 [21, 25] sts, join with ss into first dc. (43 [51, 59] sts)

ROUND 9: 1ch, 1dc into each of next 20 [24, 28] sts, dc2tog three times, 1dc into each of next 17 [21, 25] sts, join with ss into first dc. (40 [48, 56] sts)

ROUND 10: 1ch, 1dc into each st of previous round, join with ss into first dc.

ROUND 11: 1ch, 1dc into each of next 22 [26, 30] sts, miss next st, 1dc into each of next 17 [21, 25] sts, join with ss into first dc. (39 [47, 55] sts)

ROUND 12: 1ch, 1dc into each of next 20 [24, 28] sts, dc3tog, 1dc into each of next 16 [20, 24] sts, join with ss into first dc. (37 [45, 53] sts)

ROUND 13: Ss into each st worked on previous round, join with ss into first ss.

Fasten off yarn

FINISHING THE SLIPPERS

Press lightly on the wrong side (Pressing, page 22). Darn the yarn ends on the wrong side using the yarn needle (Dealing With Yarn Ends, page 18).

THE BASIC MITTENS

YOU WILL NEED

- 2 [2, 2] balls of pure wool chunky yarn with approx 92m (100yds) per 100g ball
- 5.5mm (size H) and 6mm (size J) crochet hooks or sizes needed to achieve tension
- Yarn needle
- Split ring marker

FINISHED SIZE

To fit sizes Small (to fit up to 20cm/8in around hand), Medium (to fit up to 23cm/9in around hand), and Large (to fit up to 25.5cm/10in around hand). Instructions for Medium and Large sizes are given in square brackets.

TENSION

14 stitches and 16 rows to 10cm (4in) measured over double crochet worked with 6mm (size J) hook.

MAKING THE RIGHT MITTEN

Make cuff

** FOUNDATION CHAIN: Using 6mm (size J) hook, work 6 [8, 10] ch.

Change to 5.5mm (size H) hook.

FOUNDATION ROW: 1dc into 2nd ch from hook, 1dc into each ch to end, turn. (5 [7, 9] sts)

ROW 1: 1ch, working into back loops only, 1dc into first dc, 1dc into each dc to end, turn.

Rep Row 1 20 [22, 24] times more, ending with a WS row.

Work body

Change to 6mm (size J) hook.

ROW 1: 1ch, working into row ends along side edge of cuff, 2dc into first row end, 1dc into each rem row end, turn. (23 [25, 27] sts)

ROW 2: 1ch, 1dc into each dc to end, turn.

Rep Row 2 zero [2, 4] times more, ending with a WS row. **

Shape thumb gusset

ROW 1: 1ch, 1dc into each of next 13 [14, 15] dc, 2dc into next dc, 1dc into next dc, 2dc into next dc, 1dc into each of next 7 [8, 9] dc, turn. (25 [27, 29] sts)

ROW 2: 1ch, 1dc into each of next 7 [8, 9] dc, 2dc into next dc, 1dc into each of next 3dc, 2dc into next dc, 1dc into each of next 13 [14, 15] dc, turn. (27 [29, 31] sts)

ROW 3: 1ch, 1dc into each of next 13 [14, 15] dc, 2dc into next dc, 1dc into each of next 5dc, 2dc into next dc, 1dc into each of next 7 [8, 9] dc, turn. (29 [31, 33] sts)

ROW 4: 1ch, 1dc into each of next 7 [8, 9] dc, 2dc into next dc, 1dc into each of next 7dc, 2dc into next dc, 1dc into each of next 13 [14, 15] dc, turn. (31 [33, 35] sts)

ROW 5: 1ch, 1dc into each of next 13 [14, 15] dc, 2dc into next dc, 1dc into each of next 9dc, 2dc into next dc, 1dc into each of next 7 [8, 9] dc, turn. (33 [35, 37] sts)

ROW 6: 1ch, 1dc into each of next 8 [9, 10] dc, 1ch (place marker in ch), miss next 11dc, 1dc into each of next 14 [15, 16] dc, turn.

ROW 7: 1ch, 1dc into each dc and ch sp to end of row, turn. (23 [25, 27] sts)

Work even in dc for 9 [11, 13] more rows, ending with a WS row.

Shape top

*** ROW 1: 1ch, dc2tog, 1dc into each of next 7 [8, 9] dc, dc2tog, 1dc into next dc, dc2tog, 1dc into each of next 7 [8, 9] dc, dc2tog, turn. (19 [21, 23] sts)

ROW 2: 1ch, 1 dc into each dc, turn.

ROW 3: 1ch, dc2tog, 1dc into each of next 5 [6, 7] dc, dc2tog, 1dc into next dc, dc2tog, 1dc into each of next 5 [6, 7] dc, dc2tog, turn. (15 [17, 19] sts)

ROW 4: Rep Row 2.

ROW 5: 1ch, dc2tog, 1dc into each of next 3 [4, 5] dc, dc2tog, 1dc into next dc, dc2tog, 1dc into each of next 3 [4, 5] dc, dc2tog, turn. (11 [13, 15] sts)

Fasten off yarn.

Work thumb

With RS of work facing and 6mm (size J) hook, rejoin yarn with ss to marked ch.

ROUND 1: 1ch, 1dc into same sp as ss, 1dc into each dc; join with ss to first dc. (12 [12, 12] sts)

Rep Round 1 six [8, 10] times more.

NEXT ROUND: 1ch, dc2tog six times. (6 [6, 6] sts)

Fasten off yarn leaving 20cm (8in) tail. Thread tail in yarn needle, draw through rem sts and fasten off tightly.***

MAKING THE LEFT MITTEN

Work as given for right mitten from ** to **.

Shape thumb gusset

ROW 1: 1ch, 1dc into each of next 7 [8, 9] dc, 2dc into next dc, 1dc into next dc, 2dc into next dc, 1dc into each of next 13 [14, 15] dc, turn. (25 [27, 29] sts)

ROW 2: 1ch, 1dc into each of next 13 [14, 15] dc, 2dc into next dc, 1 dc into each of next 3dc, 2dc into next dc, 1dc into each of next 7 [8, 9] dc, turn. (27 [29, 31] sts)

ROW 3: 1ch, 1dc into each of next 7 [8, 9] dc, 2dc into next dc, 1dc into each of next 5dc, 2dc into next dc, 1dc into each of next 13 [14, 15] dc, turn. (29 [31, 33] sts)

ROW 4: 1ch, 1dc into each of next 13 [14, 15] dc, 2dc into next dc, 1dc into each of next 7dc, 2dc into next dc, 1dc into each of next 7 [8, 9] dc, turn. (31 [33, 35] sts)

ROW 5: 1ch, 1dc into each of next 7 [8, 9] dc, 2dc into next dc, 1dc into each of next 9dc, 2dc into next dc, 1dc into each of next 13 [14, 15] dc, turn. (33 [35, 37] sts)

ROW 6: 1ch, 1dc into each of next 15 [16, 17] dc, 1ch (place marker in ch), miss next 11dc, 1dc into each of next 7 [8, 9] dc, turn.

ROW 7: 1ch, 1dc into each dc and ch sp to end of row, turn. (23 [25, 27] sts)

Work in dc for 9 [11, 13] more rows, ending with a WS row.

Work as given for right mitten from *** to ***.

FINISHING THE MITTENS

Press the mittens lightly on the wrong side (Pressing, page 22). Darn the yarn ends on the wrong side using the yarn needle (Dealing With Yarn Ends, page 18). With right sides together and matching yarn in the yarn needle, join the top and side seams.

chapter 2
edgings and and trimmings

From **pompoms** and **fringes** to **tassels** and **flower trims**, Chapter 2 covers a wide range of easy-to-apply edgings and decorations. The humble granny square is brought bang up-to-date and put into service as a funky pocket on Jazz, a hot pink scarf. Gloriously **frilled cuffs** turn a pair of plain mittens into a flirty, girly creation called Florence. Crochet edgings feature in this chapter, from the pretty **shell edging** on Priscilla to the smart and stylish edging on College.

susie

narrow scarf with pompoms

An edging of shaggy pompoms makes a narrow scarf into a fun accessory. Add one pompom to each corner and space the others at regular intervals along the edges, leaving a short length of yarn between pompom and crochet so the pompoms hang down gracefully.

YOU WILL NEED

- 2 balls of pure wool DK yarn with approx 125m (137yd) per 50g ball in main colour
- 3 balls of the same yarn in contrasting colour
- 6mm (US size J) and 6.5mm (US size K) crochet hooks or sizes needed to achieve tension
- Yarn needle

FINISHED SIZE

Scarf measures 7cm (2³⁄₄in) wide and 114cm (45in) long.

TENSION

12 stitches and 6 rows to 10cm (4in) measured over treble crochet using 6mm (US size J) hook and two strands of main yarn held together.

WORKING THE SCARF

Crochet and finish the scarf following the basic pattern on page 24, but begin with a foundation chain of 11 instead of 22. Work in treble crochet until the scarf measures 114cm (45in) long.

MAKING AND APPLYING THE POMPOMS

1 Using 2 strands of contrasting yarn held together, wind yarn between fixed points (see Tip) to make a hank of approximately 100 strands.

2 Cut 140cm (55in) lengths of main yarn (you'll need 22 lengths, 1 for tying each pompom). Fold a length of cut yarn in half and tie it around centre of hank in a square knot.

3 Fold yarn ends around hank and knot once again to secure. Repeat at 8cm (3in) intervals along hank.

4 Remove tied hank from fixed points and lay flat. Cut through hank between yarn ties with sharp scissors. Take care not to cut through ties by mistake. Repeat Steps 1-4 until you have made 22 pompoms.

5 Fluff out ends of pompoms, trimming off any straggly yarn ends. Use ties threaded in yarn needle to attach a pompom to each corner of scarf, leaving about 2.5cm (1in) of tie between pompom and scarf. Attach 9 pompoms to each long edge of scarf, spacing them evenly along edge, and adding 1 to each corner.

Tip

The scarf is worked with two strands of DK yarn in main colour held together throughout. When winding the yarn to make the pompoms, you need two fixed points approximately 76cm (30in) apart, such as two cupboard door knobs or two quick-release clamps fixed to a table.

priscilla

scarf with shell edging

A row of simple shell edging makes a pretty, contrasting trim at each end of a scarf. Start by working a few rows of double crochet into the edge first, to make a firm foundation for the shells, using the same weight of yarn as the scarf.

YOU WILL NEED

- 2 balls of pure wool chunky yarn in main colour with approx 92m (100yd) per 100g ball
- Oddments of the same yarn in contrasting colour
- 5.5mm (US size I), 6mm (US size J), and 6.5mm (US size K) crochet hooks or sizes needed to achieve tension
- Yarn needle

FINISHED SIZE

Scarf measures 15cm (6in) wide and 102cm (40in) long, not including edging.

TENSION

12 stitches and 6 rows to 10cm (4in) over treble crochet using 6mm (US size J) hook or size needed to achieve tension.

WORKING THE SCARF

Crochet and finish the scarf following the basic pattern on page 24.

Prefer the slippers? **see page 27 for the basic pattern**

WORKING THE EDGING

1 Using 5.5mm (US size I) hook, join contrasting yarn to right side of scarf end. Chain 1, then work 2 double crochet into first stitch. Continue along row, working 1 double crochet into each stitch along end of scarf. (21 dc)

2 Turn at end of row, chain 1 and work 1 double crochet into each stitch of previous row.

3 Turn, chain 1 and work 1 double crochet into first stitch. *Skip next 2 stitches and work 5 treble crochet into next stitch to make a shell.

4 Finish shell by skipping next 2 stitches and working 1 double crochet into next stitch. Repeat from * to end of row. Fasten off yarn and darn in ends.

shell-edged slippers

Shell edging works well around the top of slippers. Omit the row of slip stitches in the basic pattern and work the edging directly into the top of the slippers using a contrasting yarn colour.

jazz

scarf with granny square pockets

Brighten up a plain scarf by adding a granny square pocket to each end. Work the pockets in the main yarn plus a contrasting yarn or work each round in a different colour for extra effect.

YOU WILL NEED

- 2 balls of pure wool chunky yarn in main colour (MC) with approx 92m (100yd) per 100g ball
- Oddments of the same yarn in a contrasting colour (CC)
- 6mm (US size J) and 6.5mm (US size K) crochet hooks or sizes needed to achieve tension
- Yarn needle

FINISHED SIZE

Scarf measures 15cm (6in) wide and 102cm (40in) long. Pocket measures 15cm (6in) square.

TENSION

12 stitches and 6 rows to 10cm (4in) measured over treble crochet using 6mm (US size J) hook, or size needed to achieve this tension.

WORKING THE SCARF

Crochet and finish the scarf following the basic pattern on page 24.

Working the pockets (make two)

YARN: Worked in two colours, MC and CC.

FOUNDATION RING: Using CC, 6ch and join with ss to form a ring.

ROUND 1: 3ch (counts as 1tr), 2tr into ring, 3ch, *3tr into ring, 3ch; rep from * twice more, join with ss into 3rd of 3ch. Break off CC.

ROUND 2: Join MC to any 3ch sp, 3ch (counts as 1tr), [2tr, 3ch, 3tr] into same sp (corner made), *1ch, [3tr, 3ch, 3tr] into next 3ch sp; rep from * twice more, 1ch, join with ss into 3rd of 3ch. Break off MC.

ROUND 3: Join CC to any 3ch corner sp, 3ch (counts as 1tr), [2tr, 3ch, 3tr] into same sp, *1ch, 3tr into ch sp, 1ch, **[3tr, 3ch, 3tr] into next 3ch corner sp; rep from

* twice and from * to ** once again, join with ss into 3rd of 3ch. Break off CC.

ROUND 4: Join MC to any 3ch corner sp, 3ch (counts as 1tr), [2tr, 3ch, 3tr] into same sp, *[1ch, 3tr] into each ch sp along side of square, 1ch, **[3tr, 3ch, 3tr] into next 3ch corner sp; rep from * twice and from * to ** once again, join with ss into 3rd of 3ch.

ROUND 5: 1ch, 1dc into same place as ss, 1dc into each tr on previous round, working 3dc into each 3ch sp and 1dc into each ch sp, join with ss into first dc. Fasten off yarn and darn in all ends.

MAKING THE POCKETS

1 Using contrasting yarn, work foundation ring and Round 1. Join the round by working a slip stitch through third of three starting chains and fasten off yarn.

2 Join main yarn to any chain space worked on Round 1 by placing a slip knot on hook, inserting it into chain space and working a slip stitch to secure the new yarn.

3 Work corners on Rounds 2, 3 and 4 by working 2 groups of 3 treble crochet stitches separated by 3 chains into each corner space worked on the previous round.

4 On final round, work 1 double crochet stitch into each stitch made on previous round. As you proceed around square, work 3 double crochet stitches into each corner space and 2 double crochet stitch into each of smaller spaces along sides.

5 Pin 1 finished square to each end of scarf. Oversew 3 sides of each square onto scarf to make pockets, working stitches through outer loops of final row of stitches around squares.

pocket bag

A granny square makes an unusual yet practical pocket for a buttonhole bag. Pin the pocket in place and use matching yarn to backstitch the sides and lower edge of the square to the bag, taking each stitch through both loops of the final round of the square.

summer

bag with crochet flower trim

Stitching chunky crochet flowers onto a cream buttonhole bag is a quick way to add a summery look to a plain crocheted surface. Choose bright yarn colours to make the flowers and stitch each one securely in place using the yarn tail.

YOU WILL NEED

- 4 balls of pure wool DK yarn with approx 125m (137yd) per 50g ball in main colour
- Oddments of chunky yarn in 3 contrasting colours
- 5.5mm (US size I), 6mm (US size J), and 6.5mm (US size K) crochet hooks or sizes needed to achieve tension
- Yarn needle

FINISHED SIZE

Bag measures 24cm (9^1/$_2$in) deep, including handles, and 28cm (11 in) wide. Flowers are approximately 8cm (3in) in diameter.

TENSION

14 stitches and 16 rows to 10 cm (4in) measured over double crochet using 6mm (US size J) hook and two strands of main yarn held together.

NOTE

The bag is worked with two strands of DK yarn held together throughout; the flowers are worked with one strand of chunky yarn.

WORKING THE BAG

Crochet the bag front and back pieces following the basic pattern on page 25.

WORKING THE FLOWERS
(make four)

YARN: Worked in 3 contrasting colours.

FOUNDATION RING: Using first colour and 5.5mm (US size I) hook, ch 6 and join with sl st to form a ring.

ROUND 1: Ch 3 (counts as 1 tr), 14 tr into ring, join with sl st into 3rd of ch-3. Break off first colour.

ROUND 2: Join second colour to any tr, 1 dc into same st, *3 tr into each of next 2 tr, 1 dc into next tr; rep from * to last 2 sts, 3 tr into each of last 2 tr, join with sl st into first dc.

Fasten off yarn, leaving a long tail. Darn in all other yarn ends except for the long tail. Make 2 flowers using the same colour combination and 2 flowers using first colour at the centre and third colour for the petals.

WORKING THE FLOWERS

1 Using first colour, work foundation ring and Round 1. Join the round by working a slip stitch through third of 3 starting chains and fasten off yarn. Join second colour to any stitch worked on Round 1 by inserting hook into stitch and pulling loop of new yarn through it.

2 With new yarn, work 1 slip stitch then 1 double crochet into same stitch.

3 Work 3 treble crochet into each of next 2 stitches to make first petal.

4 Work 3 more petals around motif, leaving 2 stitches remaining. Work 3 treble crochet into each of these stitches, then join the round by working 1 slip stitch into first double crochet of round.

5 Using photograph as guide, pin finished flowers to front of bag. Using yarn tails, stitch each flower to bag, taking 2 or 3 small stitches between each petal, and stitching through both flower and bag. Secure yarn neatly on wrong side.

FINISHING THE BAG

Finish the bag as given in the basic pattern on page 25.

arizona

bag with yarn fringe

A simple fringe makes a great finishing touch along the bottom edge of a bag. You can use the same yarn as the bag or give a different look by making the fringe in another colour or texture of yarn. Making a fringe is a great opportunity to use up yarn oddments from your stash.

YOU WILL NEED

- 2 balls of pure wool chunky yarn with approx 92m (100yd) per 100g ball
- 6mm (US size J) and 6.5mm (US size K) crochet hooks or sizes needed to achieve tension
- Yarn needle
- Piece of stiff cardboard

FINISHED SIZE

Bag measures 24cm (9$\frac{1}{2}$in) deep, not including fringe, and 28cm (11in) wide.

TENSION

14 stitches and 16 rows to 10cm (4in) measured over double crochet using 6mm (US size J) hook or size needed to achieve tension.

WORKING THE BAG

Crochet and finish the bag following the basic pattern on page 25.

MAKING THE FRINGE

1 Decide how deep finished fringe will be and cut a rectangle of cardboard to same depth plus 2.5cm (1in). Wind yarn evenly around cardboard and cut along bottom edge to make strands.

2 Insert larger crochet hook from back to front of lower edge of bag. Gather 3 strands into a group, fold in half and loop fold over hook.

3 Carefully pull hook and folded yarn through to wrong side of bag to make loop.

4 Loop hook around cut ends of yarn group and pull gently through to complete tassel. Repeat at regularly spaced intervals along bag edge. Neaten by trimming any long strands.

Prefer the scarf? **see page 24 for the basic pattern**
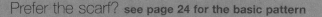

fringed scarf

A classic fringe finishes off the ends of a scarf nicely. You can make the fringe any length you like, but for best results be generous with the number of strands you use in each group.

fluffy

shortie mittens with marabou trim

Short, wrist-skimming mittens look great with a fancy edging. It's easy to stitch lengths of brightly coloured marabou trim around the cuff, but remember to remove it before washing the mittens.

YOU WILL NEED

- 2 [2, 2] balls of pure wool chunky yarn with approx 92m (100yd) per 100g ball
- 6mm (US size J) and 6.5mm (US size K) crochet hooks or sizes needed to achieve tension
- Yarn needle
- Split ring marker
- Sewing thread to match yarn colour
- Narrow marabou trim in a contrasting colour, approx 25 [29, 33]cm (10 [11$\frac{1}{2}$, 13]in) for each mitten
- Sewing needle

FINISHED SIZES

To fit sizes Small (to fit up to 20cm/8in around hand), Medium (to fit up to 23cm/9in around hand), and Large (to fit up to 25.5cm/10in around hand). Instructions for Medium and Large sizes are given in square brackets.

TENSION

14 stitches and 16 rows to 10cm (4in) measured over double crochet using 6mm (US size J) hook or size needed to achieve tension.

Prefer the bag? see page 25 for the basic pattern

WORKING THE MITTENS

Using 6.5mm (US size K) hook, ch 24 [26, 27]. Change to 6mm (US size J) hook.

ROW 1: 1 dc into 2nd ch from hook, 1 dc into each ch to end, turn.

(23 [25, 26] sts)

ROW 2: Ch 1, 1 dc into each dc to end, turn.

Rep Row 2 another 2 [2, 4] times, ending with a WS row.

Change to following the basic pattern on pages 28–29, working from "Shape thumb gusset" to end.

Finish mittens as given in basic pattern.

glamorous bag

Marabou trim adds a touch of femininity to a plain pink bag with grab handles. Choose a strongly contrasting colour for the trim and position it along the top edge as shown or stitch it around the other three sides as well for a bolder effect.

APPLYING MARABOU TRIM

1 Pin marabou trim around right side of cuff edge of mitten, starting at seam and inserting pins at right angles to edge of crochet.

2 When trim is pinned all the way around, overlap ends of trim by about 2cm (³/₄in) and cut off surplus.

3 Working from inside of mitten, stitch trim down by sewing core of it carefully to right side of crochet using sewing thread that matches yarn colour. Take stitches through trim at right angles to core, taking care to pull any caught feathers free when making each stitch.

4 Take care when sewing section of trim that overlaps, making sure you catch both ends of trim in with stitches. Secure thread ends neatly on wrong side.

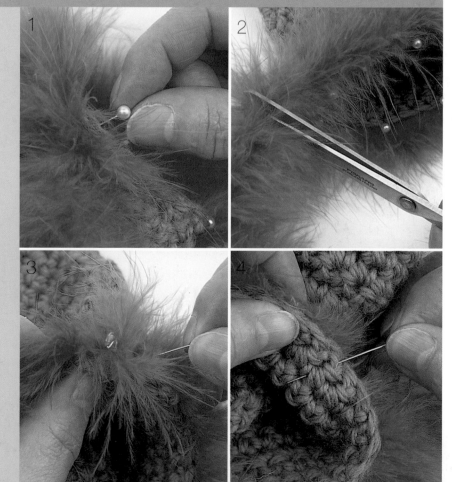

florence

mittens with frilled cuff

Make a pair of shortie mittens without cuffs and edge them with delicately fluted frills. Use two strands of yarn for the mittens and one matching strand for the frills, or make the mittens in chunky yarn with contrasting frills in thinner yarn.

YOU WILL NEED

- 3 balls of pure wool DK yarn with approx 125m (137yd) per 100g ball
- 4mm (US size F), 6mm (US size J), and 6.5mm (US size K) crochet hooks or sizes needed to achieve tension
- Yarn needle

FINISHED SIZE

To fit sizes Small (to fit up to 20cm/8in around hand), Medium (to fit up to 23cm/9in around hand), and Large (to fit up to 25.5cm/10in around hand). Instructions for Medium and Large sizes are given in square brackets. Frill measures 4cm (1^1/2in) deep for all sizes.

TENSION

14 stitches and 16 rows to 10cm (4in) measured over double crochet using 6mm (US size J) hook and two strands of yarn held together.

NOTE

The mittens are worked with two strands of yarn held together throughout; the frills are worked with one strand of yarn.

WORKING THE MITTENS

FOUNDATION CHAIN: Using 6.5mm (US size K) hook, ch 24 [26, 28]. Change to 6mm (US size J) hook.

FOUNDATION ROW: (RS) 1 dc into 2nd ch from hook, 1 dc into each ch to end, turn. (23 [25, 27] dc)

ROW 1: Ch 1, 1 dc into each dc of previous row, turn.

Rep Row 1 another 3 [5, 7] more times, ending with a WS row.

Finish working the mittens by following the basic pattern on pages 28–29 from 'Shape thumb gusset', making sure you work one right and one left mitten.

MAKE FRILL

With RS of mitten facing, join yarn to cuff edge with one strand of yarn and 4mm (US size F) hook.

ROW 1: Ch 3 (counts as 1 tr), 2 tr into first st, 3 tr into each st to end, turn. (69 [75, 81] tr)

ROW 2: Ch 3, 1 tr into each tr of previous row, turn.

ROW 3: Ch 3 (counts as 1 tr), 1 tr into first st, 2 tr into each tr of previous row. (138 [150, 162] tr)

Fasten off yarn.

Prefer the scarf? see page 24 for the basic pattern

MAKING THE FRILL

1 Make a slip knot in 1 strand of yarn and put it on 4mm (US size F) hook. With right side of mitten facing and cuff edge uppermost, insert hook into edge, wrap yarn over hook and make a slip stitch to join yarn.

2 Beginning with turning chain and 2 treble crochet stitches worked into first stitch, work 3 treble crochet stitches into each stitch along mitten edge and turn.

3 On next row, begin with turning chain and work 1 treble crochet stitch into each stitch of previous row and turn.

4 On final row, begin with turning chain and 1 treble crochet stitch worked into first stitch. Work 2 treble crochet stitches into each remaining stitch of previous row.

FINISHING THE MITTENS
Finish the mittens as given in the basic pattern on pages 28–29.

frilled scarf

Make a narrow scarf in two strands of yarn, beginning with eleven chains and working in treble crochet. Using one strand of yarn, work three double crochet stitches into each row end down the long sides of the scarf, then work the frill as above. Finish off the edge of each frill with a row of double crochet worked in a contrasting colour.

college

hat with crab stitch edging

Crab stitch edging makes a firm, corded edge for a plain hat. Unlike most other crochet techniques, the edging is worked from left to right along the round or row.

YOU WILL NEED

- 1 ball of pure wool chunky yarn in main colour (MC) with approx 92m (100yd) per 100g ball
- Small amount of the same yarn in contrasting colour (CC)
- 5.5mm (US size I), 6mm (US size J), and 6.5mm (US size K) crochet hooks or sizes needed to achieve tension
- Yarn needle

FINISHED SIZE

Hat measures 20cm (8in) deep, not including edging, and 56cm (22in) in circumference and will fit average adult head.

TENSION

12 stitches and $6\frac{1}{2}$ rows to 10cm (4in) measured over treble crochet using 6mm (US size J) hook.

MAKING THE HAT

Crochet and finish the hat following the basic pattern on page 26.

WORKING THE EDGING

1 Make a slip knot in contrasting yarn and put it on 5.5mm (US size I) hook. Insert hook into hat edge close to where rounds join. Wrap yarn over hook and make a slip stitch to join yarn, then work 1 chain.

2 Working from left to right with yarn at back of work, insert hook from front to back into next stitch on right.

3 Wrap yarn over hook and draw loop through from back to front so there are now 2 loops on hook.

4 Wrap yarn over hook, then draw yarn through both loops to complete stitch.

5 Continue to work from left to right, repeating Steps 1, 2, and 3 around edge of hat and joining round with a slip stitch into first stitch.

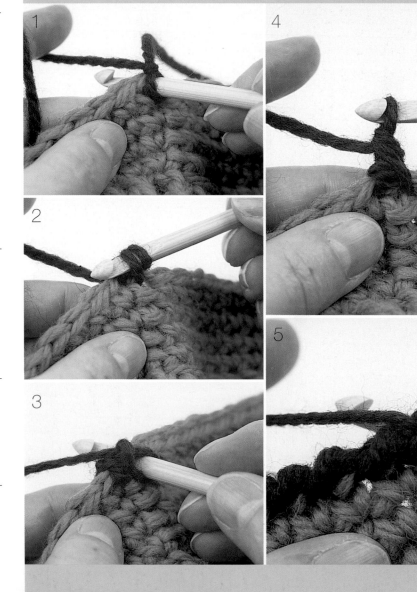

Prefer the slippers? **see page 27 for the basic pattern**

edged slippers

Make a pair of slippers using a solid colour of yarn, omitting the last round, and fasten off the yarn. Using a contrasting, variegated yarn, work a row of crab stitch edging around each slipper.

topknot

hat with crochet tassel

One large, generous tassel made from crochet chain loops decorates the crown of this hat. This type of tassel is made in a strip, then the base is rolled up and stitched to secure before being applied to the hat.

YOU WILL NEED

- 1 ball of pure wool chunky yarn with approx 92m (100yd) per 100g ball
- 6mm (US size J) and 6.5mm (US size K) crochet hooks or sizes needed to achieve tension
- Yarn needle

FINISHED SIZE

Hat measures 20cm (8in) deep, not including tassel, and 56cm (22in) in circumference and will fit average adult head. Tassel measures 15cm (6in) long.

TENSION

12 stitches and $6\frac{1}{2}$ rows to 10cm (4in) measured over treble crochet using 6mm (US size J) hook or size needed to achieve tension.

MAKING THE HAT

Crochet the hat following the basic pattern on page 26.

WORKING THE TASSEL

1 Using 6mm (US size J) hook and leaving 30-cm (12-in) yarn tail, make foundation chain of 15 chains and work 4 rows of double crochet. Turn, chain 1 and work 1 double crochet into first stitch.

2 Work 1 double crochet into next stitch and work 30 chains.

3 To close chain into a loop, work a slip stitch into double crochet just worked.

4 Repeat Steps 2 and 3 until there are 9 loops in row, then work 1 double crochet into each of 4 remaining stitches. Fasten off yarn, leaving yarn tail as before.

5 Starting at end without loops, roll crochet strip into tight coil, making sure starting tail is free.

6 Thread ending tail into yarn needle and stitch end of coil in place. Use same tail to work several stitches across end of coil and bring it through near starting tail.

FINISHING THE HAT

Finish the hat following the basic pattern on page 26. Use the yarn tails to stitch the tassel to the crown of the hat.

loopy

hat with looped edging

A pretty crochet edging is made from loops of chain stitches joined at intervals to the edge of the hat. Make the edging in the same yarn as the hat or use a brightly contrasting yarn of similar weight instead.

YOU WILL NEED

- 1 ball of pure wool chunky yarn with approx 92m (100yd) per 100g ball
- 5.5mm (US size I), 6mm (US size J), and 6.5mm (US size K) crochet hooks or sizes needed to achieve tension
- Yarn needle

FINISHED SIZE

Hat measures 20cm (8in) deep, not including edging, and 56cm (22in) in circumference and will fit average adult head.

TENSION

12 stitches and $6^{1/2}$ rows to 10cm (4in) measured over treble crochet using 6mm (US size J) hook or size needed to achieve tension.

MAKING THE HAT

Crochet the hat following the basic pattern on page 26, but don't break off the yarn.

Prefer the scarf? **see page 24 for the basic pattern**

WORKING THE EDGING

1 After joining last round of hat with a slip stitch, change to 5.5mm (US size I) hook and work 1 chain, then work 1 double crochet stitch into same stitch as slip stitch.

2 Work 6 chains, skip next 3 stitches and insert hook into fourth stitch.

3 Work 1 double crochet stitch into fourth stitch and another into next stitch. Continue around hat, working 6 chains, skipping 3 stitches and working a double crochet stitch into each of next 2 stitches.

4 End last repeat with 1 double crochet stitch then join round by working a slip stitch into first double crochet stitch.

FINISHING THE HAT
Finish the hat following the basic pattern on page 26.

looped scarf

Make the basic scarf, then trim each end with a pretty looped edging. Make each loop six chains long, and join it to the scarf edge with one double crochet stitch, spacing the loops close together along the edge.

zigzag

slippers with felt trim

Felt makes a good edging for crochet as it can be cut into shape easily, feels soft next to the skin, and doesn't fray in wear. Use pinking scissors to pattern the edges of narrow strips of felt, then stitch the felt inside the edge of the slippers.

YOU WILL NEED

- 2 [2, 3] balls of pure wool chunky yarn with approx 92m (100yd) per 100g ball
- 6mm (US size J) and 6.5mm (US size K) crochet hooks or sizes needed to achieve tension
- Yarn needle
- 23-cm (9-in) square of felt in contrasting colour
- Pinking scissors
- Sewing thread to match yarn colour
- Sewing needle

FINISHED SIZES

To fit sizes Small (to fit up to 23cm/9in sole), Medium (to fit up to 25.5cm/10in sole) and Large (to fit up to 28cm/11in sole). Instructions for Medium and Large sizes are given in square brackets.

TENSION

14 stitches and 16 rows to 10cm (4in) measured over double crochet using 6mm (US size J) hook or size needed to achieve tension.

MAKING THE SLIPPERS

Crochet and finish the slippers following the basic pattern on page 27.

APPLYING THE TRIM

1 Measure and cut out 2-cm (^{3}/$_4$-in) strips across felt square using sharp scissors. Cut enough strips to fit around edge of each slipper, allowing for an overlap of about 1cm (^{3}/$_8$in) when joining strips.

2 Cut along 1 long edge of each felt strip with pinking scissors to make zigzag edge.

3 Pin strips inside each slipper so zigzag edge shows above slipper edge by about 5mm (^{1}/$_4$in). Stretch slipper edge slightly while pinning strips to allow crochet to stretch slightly in wear.

4 Join strips by overlapping them by about 1cm (^{3}/$_8$in), cutting strips to fit where necessary.

5 Stitch strips in place using matching sewing thread in sewing needle. Working from right side and taking care to go through both layers, make row of neat running stitches below slip stitch edge of slipper.

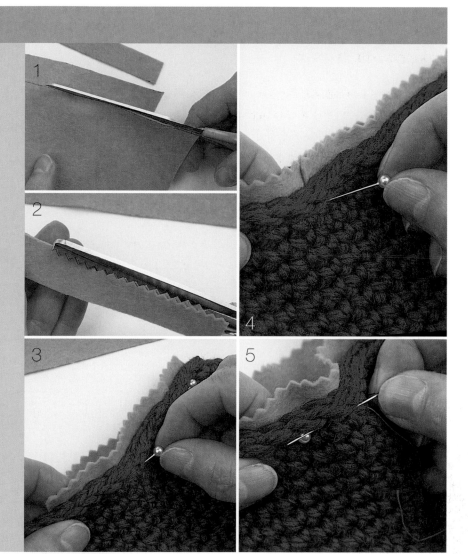

felt-trimmed bag

Pinked felt strips make a pretty decoration for the edge of a plain bag. If you choose an acrylic felt, the trim can be washed with the bag and won't shrink. Trimmings made from pure wool felt will shrink and should always be removed before washing.

Tip
Make sure you choose washable, non-shrink felt for trimming your slippers. Otherwise, the decorative edge will shrink and you may not be able to fit into your slippers any more!

fastenings and handles

This chapter features over a dozen fabulous ideas for using a wide range of both **handmade** and **store-bought** handles and fastenings. Crocheted and **braided ties** transform a plain hat into a great winter accessory that you might like to combine with the bag with braided fastenings. **Bamboo handles** make a terrific closure for a chunky bag, and **ball buttons** and **crochet loops** make pretty fastenings for our Copper scarf. Brightly coloured **zips** add a striking, punk touch to the Snappy mittens and buttonhole bag, while the basic slippers become sporty footwear thanks to the addition of **tab fastenings**.

copper

scarf with ball buttons and loops

Crochet a short scarf and make button loops along one edge of it. Cover large wooden beads with crochet to make decorative ball buttons, sew them on the opposite edge of the scarf and fasten to make a cosy muffler.

YOU WILL NEED

- 4 balls of pure wool DK yarn with approx 125m (137yd) per 50g ball
- 4mm (US size F), 6mm (US size J), and 6.5mm (US size K) crochet hooks or sizes needed to achieve tension
- Yarn needle
- Split stitch markers
- 3 wooden beads, each 2cm (³/₄in) in diameter

FINISHED SIZE

Scarf measures 16cm (6¹/₄in) wide and 110cm (43in) long.

TENSION

12 stitches and 6 rows to 10cm (4in) over treble crochet using 6mm (US size J) hook and two strands of yarn held together.

NOTE

The scarf is worked in two strands of yarn held together. Ball buttons are worked with one strand of the same yarn.

WORKING THE SCARF

Crochet and finish the scarf following the basic pattern on page 24, working until the scarf measures 43in. (110cm) long.

button and loop bag

A chunky ball button and loop make a secure fastening for a buttonhole bag. Make button and loop in contrasting yarn and position them in the centre of the buttonhole edge, directly beneath the handle.

Prefer the bag? **see page 25 for the basic pattern**

MAKING THE BUTTONS AND LOOPS

1 Using 4mm (US size F) hook and single strand of yarn, chain 2, then work 4 double crochet into first chain. Without joining the round, work 2 double crochet into each of the 4 stitches made on previous round.

2 Continue working in double crochet, shaping cover by working 2 double crochet stitches into every alternate stitch until piece is large enough to cover half of bead.

3 Place cover on bead and start decreasing. Work 1 double crochet into next stitch then work next 2 stitches together. Repeat until bead is almost covered, then work every 2 stitches together until cover is complete.

4 Fasten off yarn, leaving tail of about 30cm (12in). Thread tail into yarn needle and work a few stitches to secure cover. Don't cut tail, because you'll need this later to sew button onto scarf.

5 Mark positions of 3 loops on wrong side of scarf. Place first marker 9 rows up from end of scarf and 2 more markers 2 rows apart.

6 Join single yarn to wrong side of scarf at marker with 4mm (US size F) hook, work 1 double crochet into scarf at same place and work loop of 8 chains. Secure loop to scarf by working 1 double crochet at second marker. Repeat to make 2 remaining loops and turn work.

7 Work chain 1, then work 1 double crochet into first stitch, 8 double crochet into first loop, and 1 double crochet into stitch between loops. Repeat to complete 3 loops, then sew buttons onto opposite edge of scarf to correspond with loops.

erica

scarf with strip closure

This short scarf fastens with an ingenious crocheted tab. Tuck the plain end of the scarf behind the tab and adjust it to get a nice snug fit around your neck.

YOU WILL NEED

- 2 balls of pure wool chunky yarn with approx 92m (100yd) per 100g ball
- Oddments of the same yarn in contrasting colour
- 5.5mm (US size I), 6mm (US size J), and 6.5mm (US size K) crochet hooks or sizes needed to achieve tension
- Yarn needle

FINISHED SIZE

Scarf measures 15cm (6in) wide and 102cm (40in) long.

TENSION

12 stitches and 6 rows to 10cm (4in) over treble crochet using 6mm (US size J) hook or size needed to achieve tension.

WORKING THE SCARF

Work and finish the scarf following the basic pattern on page 24.

Tip

To get a snug fit, make sure the strip is slightly shorter than the scarf width. Take the time to try on the scarf after you've pinned the strip in place and adjust if necessary.

MAKING THE STRIP CLOSURE

1 Using 5.5mm (US size I) hook and contrasting yarn, make a slip knot on hook 40cm (16in) from end of yarn.

2 Chain 5, then work 1 double crochet into second chain from hook. Work 1 double crochet into each remaining chain. (4 dc)

3 Turn, chain 1 and work 1 double crochet into each stitch of previous row. Repeat this row until strip reaches across width of scarf when slightly stretched. Fasten off yarn, leaving 40-cm (16-in) tail.

4 Pin strip in place about one third of way down scarf. Try scarf on to check fit and adjust position of strip if necessary.

5 Using yarn tails, stitch each end of strip to scarf and fasten off ends securely on wrong side.

TENSION

14 stitches and 16 rows to 10cm (4in) measured over double crochet using 6mm (US size J) hook or size needed to achieve tension.

WORKING THE BAG

Crochet the bag following the basic pattern on page 25 until you reach the buttonhole row, ending with a right side row. Do not break off the yarn.

orient

bag with bamboo handles

Ready-made natural bamboo handles look great with a dark green crocheted bag. However, to give the bag a different look, cut two lengths of untreated bamboo cane, paint them with dabs of colour, then seal the paint with a final coat of matte or eggshell varnish.

YOU WILL NEED

- 2 balls of pure wool chunky yarn with approx 92m (100yd) per 100g ball
- 5.5mm (US size I), 6mm (US size J), and 6.5mm (US size K) crochet hooks or sizes needed to achieve tension
- Yarn needle
- Pair of straight bamboo handles 30cm (12in) long
- Small hand saw

FINISHED SIZE

Bag measures 26.5cm (10¹/₂in) deep, including handles, and 28cm (11in) wide.

Prefer the shallow bag? **see page 25 for the basic pattern**

shallow bag

Square wooden doweling finished with two coats of matching acrylic paint makes a substantial pair of handles for a shallow bag. Make the bag as given above, but work fewer rows before making the handle strips.

ATTACHING THE HANDLES (BACK AND FRONT ALIKE)

1 To make first handle strip, change to 5.5mm (US size I) hook and continue working along top edge. Turn, chain 1 and work 1 double crochet into each of next 10 stitches.

2 Turn, chain 1 and work 1 double crochet into each of 10 stitches made on previous row. Working on these 10 stitches only, work 13 more rows of double crochet, ending with WS row. Fasten off yarn, leaving 30-cm (12-in) tail.

3 With WS of crochet facing, rejoin yarn to top edge 10 stitches in from side edge. Chain 1 and work 1 double crochet into each of 10 stitches to side edge. Working on these 10 stitches

only, work 14 more rows of double crochet to match first handle strip. Fasten off yarn leaving tail as before.

4 Lay handles across handle strips and mark the length of each handle. Handles should be about 1cm ($\frac{1}{2}$in) shorter than the width of the bag. Cut handles to size with hand saw.

5 With wrong sides of handle strips facing, fold strips in half onto wrong side of bag and pin in place. Using yarn tail, stitch end of strip to bag and stitch outside edges of strip together.

6 Slot handles into strips and stitch inside edges of strip together below each handle.

FINISHING THE BAG

Finish the bag as given in the basic pattern on page 25, ending each side seam about 1.5cm ($\frac{1}{2}$in) below the beginning of the handle strips.

hearts

bag with grab handles

Work the basic buttonhole bag without the buttonholes and attach sturdy grab handles to make a useful tote. Heart buttons stitched through both bag and handles add a decorative touch.

YOU WILL NEED

- 2 balls of pure wool Icelandic Lopi yarn with approx 100m (109yd) per 100g ball
- 5.5mm (US size I), 6mm (US size J), and 6.5mm (US size K) crochet hooks or sizes needed to achieve tension
- Yarn needle
- 4 heart-shaped buttons
- Embroidery thread to match yarn colour
- Tapestry needle

FINISHED SIZE

Bag measures 28cm (11in) deep, not including handles, and 30cm (12in) wide. Attached handles are approximately 24cm (9$\frac{1}{2}$in) long.

TENSION

11 stitches and 13 rows to 10cm (4in) measured over double crochet, using 6mm (US size J) crochet hook.

WORKING THE BAG

Omitting the buttonhole, crochet and finish the bag following the basic pattern on page 25.

MAKING THE HANDLES (make two)

With the same yarn and 5.5mm (US size I) hook, make a foundation of four chains, leaving a 38–cm (15–in) yarn tail. Work in double crochet until strip measures about 25cm (10in) ending with a right side row. Cut yarn, leaving a 38cm (15in) yarn tail, and pull tail through loop on hook to finish.

Prefer the shoulder bag? see page 25 for the basic pattern

APPLYING THE HANDLES

1 Mark position of handles on bag front. Counting along top edge of crochet, insert 2 markers, each one 8 stitches away from side edges. Markers show position of outer edge of handle.

2 Pin ends of handle to bag front, making sure top edge of front piece overlaps handle ends by about 2.5cm (1in) and outer edges of handle aligns with markers.

3 Using yarn tails, backstitch ends of handle to bag front by sewing through bag below top row of stitches. Work 2 or 3 rows of stitches to make sure handle is firmly fixed. Repeat to match on bag back.

4 With embroidery thread in a tapestry needle, secure thread on wrong side of handle by working several small stitches into crochet below backstitched line. Holding button in desired position with your thumb, bring thread to right side through both layers and through a hole in button. Take thread back through second hole in button and back to front through first hole. Make several more stitches until button is secure, then take needle through to wrong side and work 2 or 3 stitches through crochet at back of button to secure end. Repeat with remaining 3 buttons.

shoulder bag

Make and finish the bag as described left, then make double crochet shoulder strap worked on a foundation of seven chains and about 173cm (68in) long. Felt the bag and the strap separately (see pages 114 and 115 for more on felting) and allow to dry. Stitch the ends of the strap to the bag, cutting the strap to a shorter length if necessary, and decorate with leaf-shaped buttons.

Tip

Any shape of button will work well on this plain bag. Choose sew-through type buttons and stitch them on securely, taking the stitches through both layers of crochet.

lauren

clutch bag with triangular flap

A simple triangular flap graces this version of the basic bag. Fasten the clutch bag with a pretty brooch or use one of the other fastenings in this chapter, such as a ball button and loop (Copper, page 56) or pair of crochet braids (Anna, page 70).

YOU WILL NEED

- 2 balls of pure wool chunky yarn with approx 92m (100yd) per 100g ball
- 6mm (US size J) and 6.5mm (US size K) crochet hooks or sizes needed to achieve tension
- Split stitch markers
- Yarn needle

FINISHED SIZE

Bag measures 18cm (7in) deep and 28cm (11in) wide. Flap measures approximately 10cm (4in) deep when folded over front.

TENSION

14 stitches and 16 rows to 10cm (4in) measured over double crochet using 6mm (US size J) hook or size needed to achieve tension.

WORKING THE BAG

Crochet the bag front following the basic pattern on page 25 until you have worked 25 rows of double crochet, ending with a right side row. Fasten off yarn.

Crochet the bag back in the same way, but do not break off yarn. Continue as shown at right.

Tip

Fasten the flap with a decorative pin, as shown, or change the look with one of the other fastenings shown in this chapter. To make a plain fastening, either sew a large press stud or strips of hook-and-loop tape under the flap.

WORKING THE FLAP

1 Place marker at each end of row you have just worked. Markers indicate position of top edge of front bag piece.

2 Work 3 more rows of double crochet above markers, ending with wrong side row.

3 On next row, chain 1 and start shaping flap. Decrease 1 stitch at beginning of row by working 1 double crochet into first stitch then skipping second stitch. Continue working across row in double crochet until 2 stitches remain at end of row.

4 To decrease 1 stitch at end of row, skip next stitch and work double crochet into last stitch.

5 Repeat Steps 3 and 4 on every row until 4 stitches remain, then fasten off yarn.

6 Pin front and back pieces together, right sides facing and with top edge of front piece aligning with markers on back piece. Stitch side and base seams following the method given for basic bag on page 25. After turning bag to right side, fold flap onto front and secure with brooch.

toggle

mittens with toggle fastening

Toggles make an attractive and interesting alternative to button fastenings. They are inexpensive and available in a range of colours, shapes and materials including natural wood, imitation horn and colourful plastic and resin.

Prefer the bag? **see page 25 for the basic pattern**

YOU WILL NEED

- 2 [2, 2] balls of pure wool chunky yarn with approx 92m (100yd) per 100g ball
- 5mm (US size H), 5.5mm (US size I), and 6mm (US size J) crochet hooks or sizes needed to achieve tension
- Yarn needle
- Split stitch marker
- 2 toggles with 2 holes

FINISHED SIZES

To fit sizes Small (to fit up to 20cm/8in around hand), Medium (to fit up to 23cm/9in around hand), and Large (to fit up to 25.5cm/10in around hand). Instructions for Medium and Large sizes are given in square brackets.

TENSION

14 stitches and 16 rows to 10cm (4in) measured over double crochet using 6mm (US size J) hook or size needed to achieve tension.

WORKING THE MITTENS

Crochet and finish the mittens following the basic pattern on pages 28–29 omitting sewing the cuff seam.

Tip

Toggles come in lots of shapes, sizes, and materials. Small toggles work best for fastening mittens; choose ones made from imitation horn, resin, natural wood or brightly coloured plastic.

APPLYING THE TOGGLE

1 Using 5mm (US size H) hook and leaving yarn tail of 30cm (12in), chain 10 and fasten off yarn, leaving 30-cm (12-in) tail.

2 Thread 1 yarn tail into yarn needle and thread chain through 2 holes in toggle. Gently pull chain ends so toggle sits at centre of chain and chain ends are level.

3 Following steps on page 57, make button loop on back cuff of mitten large enough to accommodate toggle.

4 Use yarn tails to stitch chain ends to front cuff of mitten, positioning toggle to correspond with loop.

toggle bag

Make a clutch bag in the same way as Lauren on page 64, but make a rectangular flap by omitting the triangular shaping and fasten it with a chunky matching toggle. The toggle on our bag has one hole, unlike the toggle on the mitten, which has two.

snappy

shortie mittens with decorative zip

Brighten up a shortie mitten by stitching a brightly coloured zip down the centre of the back. Use big, bold stitches and six strands of embroidery thread in a contrasting colour for an eye-catching effect.

YOU WILL NEED

- 2 [2, 2] balls of pure wool chunky yarn with approx 92m (100yd) per 100g ball
- 6mm (US size J) and 6.5mm (US size K) crochet hooks or sizes needed to achieve tension
- Yarn needle
- Split stitch marker
- 10-cm (4-in) lightweight dress zip in a bright colour
- Embroidery thread in contrasting colour
- Crewel needle large enough to accommodate 6 strands of embroidery thread

FINISHED SIZES

To fit sizes Small (to fit up to 20cm/8in around hand), Medium (to fit up to 23cm/9in around hand), and Large (to fit up to 25.5cm/10in around hand). Instructions for Medium and Large sizes are given in square brackets.

TENSION

14 stitches and 16 rows to 10cm (4in) measured over double crochet using 6mm (US size J) hook or size needed to achieve tension.

WORKING THE MITTENS

Using 6.5mm (US size K) hook, ch 24 [26, 27]. Change to 6mm (US size J) hook.

ROW 1: 1 dc into 2nd ch from hook, 1 dc into each ch to end, turn. (23 [25, 26] sts)

ROW 2: Ch 1, 1 dc into each dc to end, turn.

Rep Row 2 another 2 [2, 4] times, ending with a WS row.

Change to following the basic pattern on pages 28–29, working from "Shape thumb gusset" to end.

Prefer the bag? **see page 25 for the basic pattern**

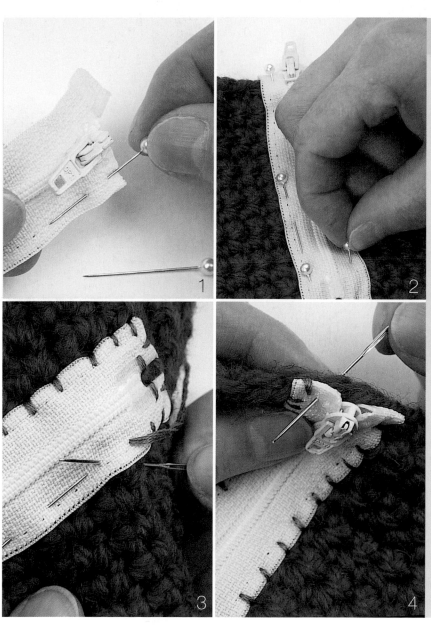

APPLYING THE ZIP

1 Turn tape edges at pull end of zip to wrong side and secure with pins.

2 On right side of mitten and with folded tape aligning with cuff edge, pin closed zip down centre of back.

3 Using 6 strands of embroidery thread in crewel needle, stitch zip in place with large straight stitches placed at right angles to zip edge.

4 To finish, work 1 or 2 stitches at either side of zip pull to secure fold to cuff edge.

FINISHING THE MITTENS
Finish the mittens as given in the basic pattern.

punk bag

Zips work well as a bag decoration. Choose lightweight dress zips in a range of contrasting colours or match the zips to the colour of the bag. For example, try black zips with shiny metal teeth against felted black or dark-coloured wool.

anna

hat with crochet braids

Crochet braids are a great way to use up odd lengths of yarn from your stash. You can crochet the chains in different colours of smooth medium-weight yarn or combine other thicknesses and textures.

YOU WILL NEED

- 2 balls of pure wool DK yarn with approx 125m (137yd) per 50g ball in main colour
- Oddments of DK yarn in 3 contrasting colours
- 4mm (US size F), 6mm (US size J), and 6.5mm (US size K) crochet hooks or sizes needed to achieve tension
- Yarn needle
- Split stitch marker

MAKING THE BRAIDS

1 Using 4mm (US size F) hook and 1 colour of contrasting yarn, make 2 lengths of chain each 175 chains long, leaving a 30-cm (12-in) yarn tail at each end. Repeat, making 2 lengths of chain with each of the 2 remaining yarn colours.

2 Mark position of braid at each side of hat with a stitch marker. Thread 3 chains (1 of each colour) through hat at marked point, using yarn needle to thread each chain separately.

3 When all 3 chains have been threaded through, adjust so ends are level. Divide with your fingers into 3 groups of 2 chains of same colour.

4 Braid chain together, working at alternate sides and moving each outside pair of chains into centre of braid. Continue braiding until about 10cm (4in) of each chain is left.

5 Tie end of braid in overhand knot, making sure knot is close to end of braiding. Darn in ends and trim excess yarn.

1

Prefer the bag? see page 25 for the basic pattern

FINISHED SIZE

Hat measures 20cm (8in) deep and 56cm (22in) in circumference and will fit average adult head. Braids measure 30cm (12in) long.

TENSION

12 stitches and 6$\frac{1}{2}$ rows to 10cm (4in) measured over treble crochet using two strands of yarn held together and 6mm (US size J) hook or size to achieve tension.

NOTE

The hat is worked with two strands of yarn in main colour held together throughout. Braids are worked with one strand of yarn.

MAKING THE HAT

Crochet and finish the hat following the basic pattern on page 26.

braided bag

Pairs of crochet braids make unusual fastenings for a bag. Make two long crochet braids as described below, attaching them to the top of a buttonhole bag at each side of the handle. Knot the braids together to fasten the bag, or make the braid a few inches longer and tie each pair in a floppy bow.

flapper

hat with earflaps

This hat is great fun to wear and gives you more than one look, depending on how you choose to wear it. Leave the earflaps and cords loose, tying the cords together under your chin to keep your ears covered, or knot them on top of your head to make a deerstalker hat.

YOU WILL NEED

- 1 ball of pure wool chunky yarn with approx 92m (100yd) per 100g ball
- 5.5mm (US size I), 6mm (US size J), and 6.5mm (US size K) crochet hooks or sizes needed to achieve tension
- Split stitch marker
- Yarn needle

FINISHED SIZE

Hat measures 20cm (8in) deep and 56cm (22in) in circumference and will fit average adult head.

TENSION

12 stitches and 6$\frac{1}{2}$ rows to 10cm (4in) measured over treble crochet using 6mm (US size J) hook or size needed to achieve tension.

MAKING THE HAT

Crochet and finish the hat following the basic pattern on page 26.

Tip

If you want to make longer earflaps than shown, work a few more rows of crochet at the start of each flap before beginning the shaping.

MAKING THE EARFLAPS

1 Try on finished hat and mark positions of front of earflaps with markers. Take off hat and insert markers for back of each earflap into eighth stitch back from first markers.

2 With right side of hat facing and using 5.5mm (US size I) hook, join yarn into stitch at right marker. Chain 1 and work 1 double crochet into same stitch.

3 Work 1 double crochet into each stitch up to left marker. Working on these 9 stitches only, work 7 more rows of double crochet, ending with wrong side row.

4 Shape lower part of earflap. Work chain 1, work first 2 double crochet stitches together, continue in double crochet until 2 stitches remain, work these 2 stitches together. Repeat this row twice more until 3 stitches remain.

5 Work chain 1, then work 3 stitches together to leave 1 stitch on hook. Working on this stitch, chain 30 and fasten off yarn, leaving 18-cm (7-in) tail.

6 Cut 6 lengths of yarn 36cm (14in) long. Thread 3 strands in yarn needle and through last chain. Tie strands in overhand knot just below end of chain and trim yarn ends to make neat tassel.

sporty

slippers with tab fastening

Give your slippers a sporty look by making a tab fastening across the instep. Fasten the tabs with squares of hook-and-loop tape so they are a snug fit without being too tight.

YOU WILL NEED

- 2 [2, 3] balls of pure wool chunky yarn with approx 92m (100yd) per 100g ball
- 5.5mm (US size I), 6mm (US size J), and 6.5mm (US size K) crochet hooks or sizes needed to achieve tension
- Yarn needle
- 2 split stitch markers
- Small piece of hook-and-loop fastening 2cm (³/₄in) wide
- Sewing thread to match yarn colour
- Sewing needle

FINISHED SIZES

To fit sizes Small (to fit up to 23cm/9in sole), Medium (to fit up to 25.5cm/10in sole) and Large (to fit up to 28cm/11in sole). Instructions for Medium and Large sizes are given in square brackets.

TENSION

14 stitches and 16 rows to 10cm (4in) measured over double crochet worked with 6mm (US size J) hook or size needed to achieve tension.

MAKING THE SLIPPERS

Crochet and finish the slippers following the basic pattern on page 27.

tab bag

Two contrasting tabs make a stylish fastening for a plain bag. Stitch one end of each tab to the buttonhole edge on the bag back and secure the other end of the tabs with hook-and-loop tape stitched onto the back of the tabs and front of the bag.

MAKING THE TABS

1 Using 5.5mm (US size I) hook, chain 5, leaving yarn tail of 30cm (12in) at beginning.

2 Work 1 double crochet into second chain from hook and 1 double crochet into each remaining chain. Continue working in double crochet on these 4 stitches until tab measures 15 [16.5, 18]cm, (6 [6$^{1}/_{2}$, 7]in). Fasten off yarn.

3 Pin chain edge of tab about halfway down each slipper towards sole. Remembering that this side of slipper goes on inside of foot, try on slippers to check tab position and adjust if necessary. Pin other ends of tabs on other sides of slippers, mark positions and remove pins.

4 Using yarn tail threaded in yarn needle, stitch chain edge of each tab securely to slippers.

5 Cut 2 squares of hook-and-loop tape. Stitch loop piece of each square onto wrong side of each tab using matching sewing thread in sewing needle. Stitch hook pieces onto right sides of slippers to correspond with markers.

chapter 4
beading and embellishing

In chapter 4 we explore the potential for adding **decorative details** to the basic patterns. All five accessories lend themselves well to the addition of **jewel trims** and **sparkling beads**, **buttons** and **novelty charms**. We show how beads can be attached to the surface of finished accessories and crocheted in. White **snowflake sequins** look fabulous arranged on a felted buttonhole bag, while chunky beads make a fun finish for a fringed scarf. In Nordic, **natural wooden buttons** transform a felted bag into a purse for every occasion. But this chapter is not just about buttons and beads: turn to page 94 for our **curlicue-trimmed** hat and scarf.

elegant

scarf with crocheted-in beads

Clear and pastel-coloured chunky beads with a sprinkling of glitter sparkle delicately against a soft green scarf. The beads are crocheted in as you work, so remember to thread them onto the yarn before you start to crochet. You might want to choose metallic beads to decorate a scarf crocheted in a richer yarn colour.

YOU WILL NEED

- 6 balls of pure wool DK yarn with approx 125m (137yd) per 50g ball
- 6mm (US size J) and 6.5mm (US size K) crochet hooks or sizes needed to achieve tension
- 128 glitter pony beads 8mm ($\frac{1}{4}$in) diameter in assorted colours
- Yarn needle small enough to pass through holes in beads

FINISHED SIZE

Scarf measures 15cm (6in) wide and 137cm (54in) long.

TENSION

14 stitches and 16 rows to 10cm (4in) over double crochet using 6mm (US size J) hook

and two strands of main yarn held together.

NOTE

The scarf is worked with two strands of DK yarn held together throughout. Bead colours are random. Thread all the beads onto the first two balls of yarn. As each ball of yarn is used up, knot the next ball onto the end and slide the beads along past the knot. When the crochet is finished, undo the knots and darn the yarn ends on the wrong side of the scarf.

WORKING THE SCARF

Work the foundation chain for the scarf following the basic pattern on page 24. Work the scarf throughout in double

crochet following the beading pattern below.

FOUNDATION ROW: (RS) 1 dc into 2nd ch from hook, 1 dc into each ch to end, turn.

ROWS 1 and 2: Ch 1, 1 dc into each dc to end, turn.

ROW 3: (WS bead row) Ch 1, 1 dc into each of next 4 dc, *add bead, 1 dc into each of next 5 dc; rep from * to last 5 sts, add bead, 1 dc into each of next 4 dc, turn.

ROWS 4, 5 and 6: Rep Row 2.

ROW 7: (WS bead row) Ch 1, 1 dc into first dc, *add bead, 1 dc into each of next 5 dc; rep from * to last 2 sts, add bead, 1 dc into last dc, turn.

ROWS 8, 9 and 10: Rep Row 2.
Rep Rows 3–10 until all beads are used, ending with a Row 6.

WORKING THE BEADING

1 Holding 2 strands of yarn together, thread beads onto both strands using suitable size of needle. Push beads down yarn for several yards to leave enough yarn to work foundation chain and first few rows of pattern.

2 On bead rows (wrong side rows), work to position of first bead. Slide bead down yarn until it rests snugly against right side of work.

3 Keeping bead in position, insert hook into bead stitch and wrap yarn around hook so there are 2 loops on hook.

4 Wrap yarn over hook again and draw it through to complete stitch. Continue adding beads in same way across row, following pattern instructions.

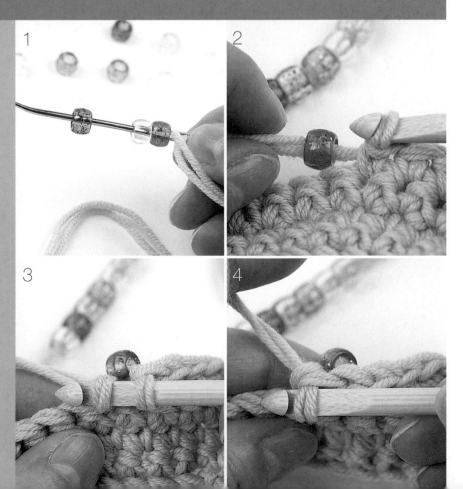

pyramid

scarf with beaded felt circles

Simple, geometric shapes work best for felt appliqué. Decorate each end of a scarf with bright circles of colour and contrasting beads, arranging the felt shapes to make a geometric pattern as shown or scatter them in a less structured way.

YOU WILL NEED

- 2 balls of pure wool chunky yarn in main colour (MC) with approx 92m (100yd) per 100g ball
- 1 ball of the same yarn in contrasting colour (CC)
- 6mm (US size J) and 6.5mm (US size K) crochet hooks or sizes needed to achieve tension
- Yarn needle
- 30-cm (12-in) square of felt
- Embroidery thread to match felt colour
- 108 decorative frosted-finish beads in a contrasting colour
- Crewel needle small enough to go through holes in beads

FINISHED SIZE

Scarf measures 15cm (6in) wide and 102cm (40in) long.

TENSION

12 stitches and 6 rows to 10cm (4in) over treble crochet using 6mm (US size J) hook or size needed to achieve tension.

WORKING THE SCARF

Crochet and finish the scarf following the basic pattern on page 24.

Prefer the hat? **see page 26 for the basic pattern**

APPLYING THE DECORATION

1 Draw 12 circles onto felt using a cotton reel or similar object to trace around. Circles should be about 4.5cm (1³⁄₄in) in diameter. Cut out circles.

2 Pin 6 circles at each end of scarf, arranging them in a pyramid shape (as shown) or more randomly.

3 Thread 3 strands of embroidery thread in crewel needle and secure end by working a few stitches through crochet under felt. Work series of straight stitches around outside of each circle to secure it to scarf.

4 Using same thread, stitch a ring of 8 beads on each felt circle following outline of circle and making sure stitches go through felt and crochet. Finish by stitching 1 bead in centre of ring, taking thread through to wrong side to secure end.

appliqué hat

Small felt circles decorated with single beads are arranged to make a band of colour and texture around a plain hat. Make sure you use a separate length of embroidery thread to stitch down each circle so that the hat can stretch around your head.

TIP

Trim the scarf with washable felt so the decorations don't shrink when washed.

paris

scarf with beaded fringe

It's quick and easy to add gorgeous beaded fringes to scarves and other accessories. Use chunky plastic craft beads as they are light in weight, unbreakable, and come in a wide range of shapes and colours.

YOU WILL NEED

- 2 balls of pure wool chunky yarn with approx 92m (100yd) per 100g ball
- 6mm (US size J) and 6.5mm (US size K) crochet hooks or sizes needed to achieve tension
- 150 chunky transparent plastic beads in assorted shapes and colours with holes large enough to accommodate yarn
- Yarn needle

FINISHED SIZE

Scarf measures 15cm (6in) wide and 102cm (40in) long, not including the fringe.

TENSION

12 stitches and 6 rows to 10cm (4in) over treble crochet using 6mm (US size J) hook or size needed to achieve tension.

WORKING THE SCARF

Work and finish the scarf following the basic pattern on page 24.

Prefer the bag? **see page 25 for the basic pattern**

MAKING THE BEADED FRINGE

1 Cut 15 lengths of yarn, each 30-cm (24-in) long, for each end of scarf. Thread 1 length into yarn needle and insert 1 end of yarn into scarf edge.

2 Unthread needle and pull yarn through knitting until ends are level. Tie overhand knot in yarn close to scarf edge. Repeat, spacing remaining 14 lengths evenly along edge.

3 Thread 1 bead onto 1 strand of yarn and tie overhand knot in both strands below bead to secure it. Use yarn needle to help adjust position of knots. Repeat, adding 4 more beads.

4 When all beads have been added, trim ends of yarn neatly about 2.5cm (1in) below final beads.

glitzy bag

Make the basic buttonhole bag pattern and fringe the bottom, adding colourful pink and red heart-shaped beads to make the ultimate girly accessory. The hearts are made from unbreakable plastic and come in plain, transparent, glitter and pearlized finishes.

snowflake

felted bag with sequins

Snowflake-shaped sequins add instant winter glamour to the simplest of knitted accessories. Stitch them onto a felted bag with embroidery thread, securing the centre of each sequin with a tiny bead, then work stitches across the arms of the snowflakes to hold them in place.

YOU WILL NEED

- 2 balls of pure wool Icelandic Lopi yarn with approx 100m (109yd) per 100g ball
- 6mm (US size J) and 6.5mm (US size K) crochet hooks or sizes needed to achieve tension
- Yarn needle
- Iridescent white snowflake-shaped sequins, each 2.5cm (1in) in diameter

- Size 11 seed beads to match yarn colour
- Embroidery thread to match sequin colour
- Crewel needle small enough to pass through holes in beads

FINISHED SIZE

Bag measures 25cm (10in) deep and 26cm (10$\frac{1}{4}$in) wide after felting.

TENSION

Working to an exact tension is not necessary when making a felted bag. Crochet a tension swatch using the stated hook size and machine wash it on a hot wash. The crochet fabric should feel thick and substantial and have lost some stitch definition, but still be pliable. You may need to make several swatches using different hooks to get a felted fabric that feels right. There's more information about felting on pages 114 and 115.

WORKING THE BAG

Crochet and finish the bag following the basic pattern on page 25. Felt the bag as described on pages 114 and 115.

Prefer the mittens? **see pages 28–29 for the basic pattern**

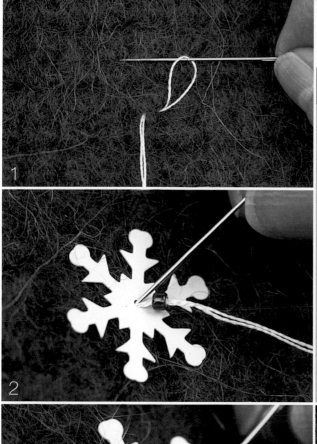

APPLYING THE SEQUINS

1 Cut a 50-cm (20-in) length of embroidery thread and divide it into single strands. Thread cut ends of 1 strand through crewel needle. On right side of bag front, take needle under 1 crochet stitch and lock thread in place by taking needle through thread loop.

2 Slide 1 snowflake sequin onto thread and take it down thread so it rests on bag. Slide a seed bead onto thread and take needle back through hole in sequin.

3 Work a short straight stitch to secure each arm of snowflake shape, then take needle through to wrong side and secure thread by working several stitches into crochet behind sequin.

4 Repeat Steps 1 to 3 to secure each snowflake sequin, scattering them at random across front of bag.

glitzy mittens

Sequins come in a huge range of shapes, sizes, and colours and they can be used to add glitz to a pair of plain mittens. Centre the sequins on the back of each mitten and stitch them securely in place with embroidery thread.

nordic

felted bag decorated with buttons

A felted bag makes the perfect surface to decorate with a selection of buttons in different shapes and sizes. Choose wooden buttons in a natural finish as shown here or use more colourful ones made from resin or plastic.

YOU WILL NEED

- 2 balls of pure wool Icelandic Lopi yarn with approx 109yd (100m) per 100g ball
- 5.5mm (US size I), 6mm (US size J), and 6.5mm (US size K) crochet hooks or sizes needed to achieve tension
- Selection of natural wood buttons
- Embroidery thread to match yarn colour
- Yarn needle

FINISHED SIZE

Bag measures 25cm (10in) deep, not including handles, and 26cm (10^1/$_4$in) wide after felting. Attached handles are approximately 30cm (12^1/$_4$in) long.

TENSION

Working to an exact tension is not necessary when making a felted bag. Crochet a tension swatch using the stated hook size and machine wash it on a hot wash. The crochet fabric should feel thick and substantial and have lost some stitch definition, but still be pliable. You may need to make several swatches using different hooks to get a felted fabric that feels right. There's more information about felting on pages 114 and 115.

WORKING THE BAG AND HANDLES

Omitting the buttonhole, crochet and finish the bag following the basic pattern on page 25. Make two grab handles (see pages 62–63) using the smallest hook and working on a foundation of five chains. Make each handle about 35cm (14in) long to allow for shrinkage. Felt the bag and the handles separately and allow to dry.

Prefer the scarf? see page 24 for the basic pattern

APPLYING THE HANDLES AND BUTTONS

1 Insert markers about 5cm (2in) from side edges of bag. Pin ends of handle to bag front so handle ends overlap top edge of bag front by about 2.5cm (1in) and outer edges of handle align with markers.

2 Using a 38–cm (15–in) length of embroidery thread in yarn needle, stitch ends of handle securely to bag front. Repeat to attach handles to bag back.

3 Thread embroidery thread into yarn needle and secure on right side of bag front by working 2 or 3 small stitches into crochet. Slot a button onto thread and slide it along thread to rest on surface of crochet.

4 Take a stitch over centre of button, going back through second hole in button and through crochet. Bring needle through first hole and make

several more stitches until button is secure, then take needle through to wrong side and work 2 or 3 stitches through crochet at back of button to secure end.

5 Repeat Steps 2, 3 and 4 to secure each button, mixing sizes and shapes of buttons and scattering them at random across bag front.

button scarf

Stitch two rows of buttons onto the ends of a plain scarf. We used heart-shaped resin buttons decorated with tartan patterns. Arrange the buttons neatly in rows, as shown, or more randomly for a fun look.

jewel

mittens with jewel trim

Plastic jewels are shiny and unbreakable and make great fun trims for crocheted accessories. Each of the square and half-moon shaped jewels used here is drilled with holes, making it easy to stitch them securely in place with matching floss. Arrange the jewels to make a neat pattern on the mitten back.

TENSION

14 stitches and 16 rows to 10cm (4in) measured over double crochet using 6mm (US size J) hook or size needed to achieve tension.

WORKING THE MITTENS

Crochet the mittens following the basic pattern on pages 28–29.

YOU WILL NEED

- 2 [2, 2] balls of pure wool chunky yarn with approx 92m (100yd) per 100g ball
- 5.5mm (US size H) and 6mm (US size J) crochet hooks or sizes needed to achieve tension
- Yarn needle
- Split stitch marker
- Embroidery thread to match yarn colour
- Plastic jewels with 2 holes: 2 x 1cm ($^3/_8$in) squares; 8 x half-moon shapes 1.5cm ($^5/_8$ in) across
- Crewel needle small enough to fit through holes in jewels

FINISHED SIZES

To fit sizes Small (to fit up to 20cm/8in around hand), Medium (to fit up to 23cm/9in around hand), and Large (to fit up to 25.5cm/10in around hand). Instructions for Medium and Large sizes are given in square brackets.

Prefer the bag? see page 25 for the basic pattern

APPLYING THE JEWELS

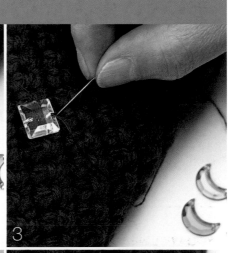

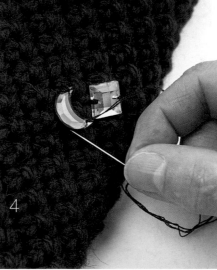

1 Cut 50-cm (20-in) length of embroidery thread and divide it into single strands. Thread cut ends of 1 strand through crewel needle. On right side of back of mitten, take needle under 1 crochet stitch and lock embroidery thread in place by taking needle through thread loop.

2 Slide 1 square jewel onto thread and take it down thread so it rests on crochet. Work 1 short stitch to secure jewel and take needle through to wrong side. Make 3 or 4 more stitches in same way.

3 Attach other side of jewel in same way. To finish, take needle through to wrong side and secure thread by working several stitches into crochet.

4 Repeat Steps 1–3 to secure each jewel, arranging them in a group to make a pleasing shape. Use a separate piece of thread for each jewel to allow mitten to stretch freely in wear.

FINISHING THE MITTENS
Finish the mittens as given in the basic pattern on pages 28–29.

hearts and stars

Scatter sparkling hearts and stars on the front of a bag crocheted with dark-coloured yarn. You can add just a few jewels as shown, or combine them with buttons and tiny bells for a more ornate look.

liberty

mittens with shells and bells

Mother-of-pearl shell rings combine well with tiny, gold-coloured liberty bells to make unusual bands of decoration on the cuffs of a pair of mittens. Take care to use a separate length of thread to stitch down each trim so the cuffs remain stretchy and comfortable to wear.

YOU WILL NEED

- 2 [2, 2] balls of pure wool chunky yarn with approx 92m (100yd) per 100g ball
- 5.5mm (US size H) and 6mm (US size J) crochet hooks or sizes needed to achieve tension
- Yarn needle
- Split ring marker
- Embroidery thread to match yarn colour
- Gold-coloured liberty bells
- Flat shell rings 2cm (^{3}/$_4$in) in diameter drilled with 1 hole
- Crewel needle small enough to fit through holes in shell rings

FINISHED SIZES

To fit sizes Small (to fit up to 20cm/8in around hand), Medium (to fit up to 23cm/9in around hand), and Large (to fit up to 25.5cm/10in around hand). Instructions for Medium and Large sizes are given in square brackets.

TENSION

14 stitches and 16 rows to 10cm (4in) measured over double crochet using 6mm (US size J) hook or size needed to achieve tension.

WORKING THE MITTENS

Crochet the mittens following the basic pattern on pages 28–29.

APPLYING THE SHELLS AND BELLS

1 Cut 50-cm (20-in) length of embroidery thread and divide it into single strands. Thread cut ends of 1 strand through crewel needle. On right side of cuff where it joins body of mitten, take needle under 1 crochet stitch and lock thread in place by taking needle through thread loop.

2 Slide 1 shell ring onto thread and take it down thread so it rests on crochet. Work 1 short stitch to secure it and take needle through to wrong side. Repeat 2 or 3 times, take needle through to wrong side and secure thread by working several stitches into crochet.

3 Repeat Steps 1 and 2 to secure each ring, arranging them at evenly-spaced intervals around cuff. Use separate piece of thread for each ring to allow cuff to stretch freely in wear.

4 Working in same way, sew 1 bell onto mitten between each shell shape.

FINISHING THE MITTENS

Finish the mittens as given in the basic pattern on pages 28–29.

molly

hat with ring buttons

A ring button is made by crocheting over a small plastic ring base. Ring buttons can be used instead of ordinary flat buttons to fasten garments, or as decorative trims on hats and other accessories. Make sure that you leave long yarn tails on the buttons since you will use them later to attach the rings to the hat.

YOU WILL NEED

- 1 ball of pure wool chunky yarn with approx 100yds (92m) per 100g ball
- Oddments of DK weight yarn in a contrasting colour
- 4mm (US size F) and 6mm (US size J) crochet hooks or sizes needed to achieve tension
- Yarn needle
- Tapestry needle with eye large enough to accommodate contrasting yarn
- 2cm (^{3}/4in) diameter plastic rings

FINISHED SIZE

Hat measures 20cm (8in) deep and 56cm (22in) in circumference and will fit average adult head.

TENSION

12 stitches and 6^1/2 rows to 10cm (4in) measured over treble crochet using 6mm (US size J) hook or size needed to achieve tension.

MAKING THE HAT

Crochet and finish the hat following the basic pattern on page 26.

Prefer the mittens? **see pages 28–29 for the basic pattern**

MAKING AND APPLYING THE BUTTONS

1 Work each ring button over a plastic ring. Using thinner yarn and 4mm (US size F) hook, make slip knot on hook and insert hook through centre of ring. Join yarn by working 1 double crochet stitch over ring.

2 Continue working around ring, making 1 round of 15 or 16 double crochet stitches over it until ring is completely covered. Join the round by working 1 slip stitch into first double crochet stitch.

3 Break off yarn, leaving end of about 38cm (15in) and thread it into tapestry needle. Work 1 row of running stitches through outer loops of crochet.

4 Turning edge of crochet backward to centre of ring, draw thread up firmly and secure it with a few stitches on wrong side, but don't break it off. Darn in short yarn end.

5 On back of button, work strands of yarn diagonally across button several times to make a shank. Bring needle to centre of button under shank.

6 Spacing buttons evenly around hat, stitch each button in place by working several stitches through centre of shank and through hat. Secure yarn end on wrong side of hat.

ring mittens

Ring buttons look attractive when arranged in a line down the back of plain mittens. Choose a smooth yarn to make buttons like the ones shown here, or use a novelty yarn incorporating metallic threads or a pretty, fluffy mohair.

curly

hat with curlicues

Six or more curlicues of crochet make a fun and unusual top knot for a hat. The curlicues are very easy to make because the spiral shape forms naturally as you crochet.

YOU WILL NEED

- 2 balls of pure wool DK yarn with approx 125m (137yd) per 100g ball
- Small amounts of the same yarn in a selection of co-ordinating colours
- 4mm (US size F), 5mm (US size H), 6mm (US size J), and 6.5mm (US size K) crochet hooks or sizes needed to achieve tension
- Yarn needle

FINISHED SIZE

Hat measures 20cm (8in) deep, not including edging, and 56cm (22in) in circumference and will fit average adult head. Plain curlicues are approximately 11cm ($4\frac{1}{4}$in) long; striped ones are 13cm (5in) long.

TENSION

12 stitches and $6\frac{1}{2}$ rows to 10cm (4in) measured over treble crochet using 6mm (US size J) hook and two strands of yarn held together.

MAKING THE HAT

Crochet and finish the hat following the basic pattern on page 26, using two strands of yarn held together.

Prefer the scarf? **see page 26 for the basic pattern**

MAKING AND APPLYING THE CURLICUES

1 Using 5mm (US size H) hook and a co-ordinating yarn, work a loose foundation chain of 30 stitches, leaving a 30–cm (12–in) yarn tail. Change to 4mm (US size F) hook and work 2 treble crochet stitches into fourth chain from hook. Work 3 treble crochet stitches into next chain.

2 Continue along chain working 3 treble crochet stitches into each chain. As you work, the crochet strip will begin to twist naturally into a curly spiral formation. At end of row, fasten off yarn and darn in yarn end.

3 To make a striped curlicue, work a plain one in one colour of yarn, leaving long ends with which to attach finished curlicue. Join a co-ordinating yarn to outer edge of top of curlicue and work a row of double crochet stitches along edge. Fasten off ends of coordinating yarn.

4 Make 3 plain and 3 striped curlicues using different shades of yarn. Attach them to crown of hat by threading yarn end of each curlicue through centre of crown and securing with a few stitches on wrong side of hat.

curly scarf

Crochet a plain scarf then decorate each end with a row of curlicues worked in a contrasting yarn colour. Space the curlicues evenly along the edge to form a chunky fringe.

charming

slippers with novelty charms

Metal charms and other jewellery components, such as rings and pendants, are useful for decorating accessories. We've chosen pretty silver strawberries and stitched a trio of them onto the front of a pair of slippers using matching thread.

YOU WILL NEED

- 2 [2, 3] balls of pure wool chunky yarn with approx 92m (100yd) per 100g ball
- 6mm (US size J) and 6.5mm (US size K) crochet hooks or sizes needed to achieve tension
- Yarn needle
- 6 silver-coloured strawberry charms approx 1.5cm (⅝ in) long
- Embroidery thread to match yarn colour
- Crewel needle small enough to go through loop on charm

FINISHED SIZES

To fit sizes Small (to fit up to 23cm/9in sole), Medium (to fit up to 25.5cm/10in sole) and Large (to fit up to 28cm/11in sole). Instructions for Medium and Large sizes are given in square brackets.

TENSION

14 stitches and 16 rows to 10cm (4in) measured over double crochet using 6mm (US size J) hook or size needed to achieve tension.

MAKING THE SLIPPERS

Crochet and finish the slippers following the basic pattern on page 27.

APPLYING THE CHARMS

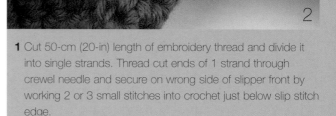

1 Cut 50-cm (20-in) length of embroidery thread and divide it into single strands. Thread cut ends of 1 strand through crewel needle and secure on wrong side of slipper front by working 2 or 3 small stitches into crochet just below slip stitch edge.

2 Bring needle through to right side at centre front, just below slip stitch edging.

3 Slide 1 charm onto thread and take it down thread so it rests flat against crochet with loop at top.

4 Take 1 stitch over loop of charm and back through crochet. Repeat 2 or 3 times until charm is securely attached and fasten off thread on wrong side by working 2 or 3 stitches into crochet.

5 Repeat Steps 1–4 to secure each charm, using separate length of thread for each charm and spacing them evenly around slipper front. Repeat on second slipper.

chapter 5
customizing crochet

In this chapter, you'll discover how **substituting yarns** and stitches can transform our five basic patterns. Try using **lacy stitch patterns**, felting the accessories, or decorating them with rows of **surface crochet** to stamp your own style on the pieces. By using some of the ideas from the earlier chapters too – changing edgings of accessories and **embellishing** them with handmade or shop-bought trimmings and handles – you can create accessories that are **entirely original** and **unique** to you.

glitter
small evening bag

It's easy to change our basic bag pattern to create a smaller accessory to use in the evening. To make this pretty evening purse, follow the basic bag pattern on page 25, working it in a thinner yarn with a smaller hook, adding contrasting stripes and leaving out the buttonhole. Add a long shoulder strap to finish the purse.

YOU WILL NEED

- 2 balls of metallic silver yarn with approx 85m (92yd) per 25g ball (MC)
- 1 ball of the same yarn in a contrasting colour (CC)
- 4mm (US size F) and 4.5mm (US size G) crochet hooks or sizes needed to achieve tension
- Yarn needle

FINISHED SIZE

Bag measures 15cm (6in) deep, not including handles, and 16cm (6¼in) wide. Attached handles are approximately 122cm (4 feet) long.

TENSION

20 stitches and 23 rows to 10cm (4in) measured over double crochet, using 4mm (US size F) hook or size needed to achieve tension.

WORKING THE BAG

Omitting the buttonhole, crochet and finish the bag following the basic pattern on page 25, working the 35 rows in this colour sequence:

18 rows in MC, 2 rows in CC, 2 rows in MC, 2 rows in CC, 2 rows in MC, 2 rows in CC, 7 rows in MC.

TIP

When working a long strip of crochet, such as a shoulder strap, make more foundation chains than you think you'll need, because the chain gets shorter when the first row of stitches are worked. Unravel any unused chains after the strap is worked.

WORKING THE SHOULDER STRAP

1 Using main yarn and 4.5mm (US size G) hook, chain length required for strap plus about one third as much again, because chain will become shorter when stitches are worked into it. (See Tip.)

2 Work 1 double crochet into second chain from hook and work along chain in double crochet until strap is desired length. Turn and work a second row of double crochet in same yarn.

3 Join contrasting yarn, turn and work 2 more rows of double crochet.

4 Join main yarn. Turn and work 2 more rows of double crochet. Fasten off yarn.

happy

stocking hat with pompoms

Give a fresh and funky new look to a basic hat by adding extra rows of treble crochet between the pattern rounds. This elongates the top section and makes a stocking cap. Trim the cap with two or more pompoms made in a contrasting yarn.

YOU WILL NEED

- 4 balls of pure wool DK yarn with approx 125m (137yd) per 50g ball in main colour
- 1 ball of the same yarn and 3 contrasting colours
- 6mm (US size J) and 6.5mm (US size K) crochet hooks or sizes needed to achieve tension
- Yarn needle
- Pompom maker (or stiff card - see Notes)

FINISHED SIZE

Hat measures 41cm (16in) deep, not including pompoms, and 56cm (22in) in circumference and will fit average adult head.

TENSION

12 stitches and $6\frac{1}{2}$ rows to 10cm (4in) measured over treble crochet using two strands of yarn held together and 6mm (US size J) hook.

NOTES

Two strands of main yarn are held together throughout. To make the pompoms, buy a set of adjustable plastic pompom rings or cut two identical doughnut shapes from sturdy card. If making your own shapes, make the centre ring about one quarter of the diameter of the outer ring.

MAKING THE HAT

Working Rounds 1–6 of the basic pattern from page 26, insert extra rows of treble crochet between the pattern rounds as follows:

Work Round 1, then work 2 rounds even.
Work Round 2, then work 3 rounds even.
Work Round 3, then work 3 rounds even.
Work Round 4, then work 3 rounds even.
Work Round 5, then work 3 rounds even.
Work Round 6, then work 3 rounds even.
Continue to follow the basic pattern from Round 7 to the end. Finish the hat as given in the basic pattern, then stitch two pompoms to the top of the hat using the yarn ties.

MAKING POMPOMS (MAKE TWO)

1 Place 2 pompom rings (or card circles) back to back. Thread several strands of yarn in yarn needle. Wind yarn around rings, adding further lengths of yarn until centre space is tightly filled.

2 Using sharp scissors, carefully cut through yarn strands, easing scissor points right between pompom rings.

3 Ease rings apart and tie length of matching yarn firmly around strands in middle of rings.

4 Pull rings apart and ease them off yarn strands. Trim off any uneven pieces of yarn. Leave yarn ties untrimmed, and use to attach pompoms to hat.

1

2

3

4

sarah

mesh tote bag

Work the basic buttonhole bag pattern in strong cotton yarn to make a useful tote bag for carrying your shopping. The central section of the bag incorporates an openwork mesh stitch, but using one of the other stitch patterns will give you a different effect.

YOU WILL NEED

- 3 balls of pure cotton DK yarn with approx 85m (92yd) per 100g ball
- 6mm (US size J) and 6.5mm (US size K) crochet hooks or sizes needed to achieve tension
- Yarn needle

FINISHED SIZE

Bag measures 30cm (12in) deep and 25cm (10in) wide.

TENSION

14 stitches and 16 rows to 10cm (4in) measured over double crochet using 6mm (US size J) hook and two strands of main yarn held together.

NOTES

Two strands of yarn are held together throughout. When working with treble yarn from an odd number of balls, you'll need to wind off half the yarn in the third ball. Make one extra stitch in the foundation chain to give the correct

number for the mesh pattern to repeat correctly.

WORKING THE BAG FRONT

Holding 2 strands of yarn together and using 6.5mm (US size K) hook, ch 34. Change to 6mm (US size J) hook and work Rows 1–4 of the basic bag pattern as given on page 25.
Start mesh pattern
ROW 1: (RS) Ch 4 (counts as 1 tr, ch 1), sk first 2 dc, 1 tr into next dc, *ch 1, sk next dc, 1 tr into next dc; rep from * to end, turn.

ROW 2: Ch 4, sk first tr, 1 tr into next tr, *ch 1, 1 tr into next tr; rep from * to end, working last tr into 3rd of ch-4, turn.
Rep Row 2 ten more times, ending with a WS row.

NEXT ROW: Ch 1, 1 dc into each ch and tr along row, working last 2 dc into 3rd and 4th of ch-4, turn.

NEXT ROW: Ch 1, 1 dc into each sc along row.

Work 3 more rows of dc, then work buttonhole and handle as given for basic pattern, but working buttonhole over 13 sts to accommodate extra chain made at beginning.

WORKING THE BAG BACK

Work as for front.

FINISHING THE BAG

Finish the bag following the basic pattern on page 25.

STITCH PATTERNS

We used the openwork mesh stitch for the bag. You can substitute either of the other two stitch patterns given here, but remember to adjust the number of stitches in the foundation chain and in the buttonhole according to the multiple of stitches required for pattern you want to work.

1 OPENWORK MESH

Work over a multiple of 2 chains plus 4.
ROW 1: (RS) 1tr into 6th ch from hook, *1ch, sk next ch, 1tr into next ch; rep from * to end, turn.
ROW 2: 4ch (counts as 1 tc, 1 ch), *1 tr into next tr, 1 ch; rep from * to end, working last tr into 2nd of beg skipped ch-5, turn.
ROW 3: 4ch (counts as 1 tr, 1 ch), *1 tr into next tr, 1 ch; rep from * to end, working last tr into 3rd of ch-4, turn.
Rep Row 3 for length required.

2 PLAIN TRELLIS

Work over a multiple of 4 chains plus 2.
ROW 1 : 1 dc into 6th ch from hook, *5ch, sk next 3 chs, 1 dc into next ch; rep from * to end, turn.
ROW 2: *5ch, 1 dc into next ch-5 sp; rep from * to end, turn.
Rep Row 2 for length required.

3 TRELLIS WITH SHELLS

Work over a multiple of 12 chains plus 3.
ROW 1: (RS) 2 tr into 4th ch from hook, *sk next 2 chs, 1 dc into next ch, 5ch, sk next 5 chs, 1 dc into next ch, sk next 2 chs, 5 tr into next ch; rep from * to end, working only 3 tr into last ch, turn.
ROW 2: 1 ch, 1 dc into first st, *5ch, 1 dc into next ch-5 sp, 5ch, 1 dc into 3rd tr of next 5-tr group; rep from * to end, working last dc into 3rd of beg skipped ch-3, turn.
ROW 3: *5ch, 1 dc into next ch-5 sp, 5 tr into next dc, 1 dc into next ch-5 sp; rep from * ending with 2ch, 1 tr into last dc, turn.
ROW 4: 1 ch, 1 dc into first st, *5ch, 1 dc into 3rd tr of next 5-tr group, 5ch, 1 dc into next ch-5 sp; rep from * to end, turn.
ROW 5: 3ch, 2 tr into first st, *1 dc into next ch-5 sp, 5ch, 1 dc into next ch-5 sp, 5 tr into next sc; rep from * to end, working only 3 tr into last dc, turn.
ROW 6: 1 ch, 1 dc into first st, *ch 5, 1 dc into next ch-5 sp, 5ch, 1 sc into 3rd tr of next 5-dc group; rep from * to end, working last dc into 3rd of ch-3, turn.
Rep Rows 3–6 for length required, ending with a Row 5.

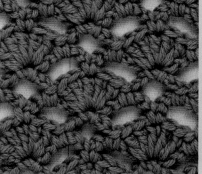

patience

lacy shell scarf

Stitch patterns need a given number of stitches in the foundation chain for the pattern to work correctly. When using a different pattern to crochet a scarf, simply chain the number required and work a long strip. The Patience scarf is worked in Lacy Shell Stitch on a foundation chain of 30 (8 x 3 + 6).

STITCHES

You can use any of the stitches shown here to make our basic scarf. Shell stitches feature groups of three or more stitches that share the same chain, stitch, or chain space, and they look rather like clam shells. Usually, chains or stitches at either side of a shell are skipped to compensate for the shell and each stitch making up a shell is counted as one stitch. Chevron stitches use a sequence of increases and decreases to create zigzag rows and look good worked in one colour or in stripes.

STITCH PATTERNS

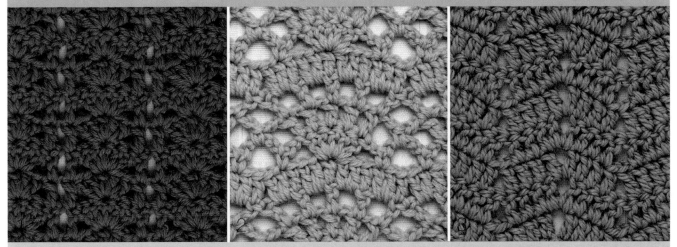

1 LACY SHELL STITCH

Work a multiple of 8 chains plus 6.

ROW 1: (RS) 1 tr into 6th ch from hook, *sk next 2 chs, 5 tr into next ch, sk next 2 chs, 1 tr into next ch, ch 1, sk next ch, 1 tr into next ch; rep from * to end, turn.

ROW 2: Ch 4 (counts as 1 tr, ch 1), sk first tr, 1 tr into next tr, *5 tr into centre st of next 5 tr group, sk next 2 tr, 1 tr into next tr, ch 1, 1 tr into next tr; rep from * working last tr into 4th of beg skipped ch-5, turn.

ROW 3: Ch 4 (counts as 1 tr, ch 1), sk first tr, 1 tr into next tr, *5 tr into centre st of next 5 tr group, sk next 2 tr, 1 tr into next tr, ch 1, 1 tr into next tr; rep from * working last tr into 3rd of ch-4, turn.

Rep Row 3 for length required.

Fasten off yarn.

2 SHELL LACE

Work a multiple of 12 chains plus 3.

ROW 1: (RS) 1 tr into 4th ch from hook, 1 tr into each ch to end, turn.

ROW 2: Ch 3, 2 tr into first tr, ch 2, sk next 3 tr, 1 dc into next tr, ch 5, sk next 3 tr, 1 dc into next tr, ch 2, sk next 3 tr, *5 tr into next tr, ch 2, sk next 3 tr, 1 dc into next tr, ch 5, sk next 3 tr, 1 dc into next tr, ch 2, sk next 3 tr; rep from * ending with 3 tr into 3rd of beg skipped ch-3, turn.

ROW 3: Ch 4, sk first tr, 1 tr into next tr, ch 1, 1 tr into next tr, ch 2, sk next ch 2 sp, 1 dc into next ch-5 sp, ch 2, *[1 tr into next tr, ch 1] 4 times, 1 tr into next tr, ch 2, sk next ch 2 sp, 1 dc into next ch-5 sp, ch 2; rep from * to last 2 tr, [1 tr into next tr, ch 1] twice, 1 tr into 3rd of ch 3, turn.

ROW 4: Ch 5, sk first tr, 1 tr into next tr, ch 2, 1 tr into next tr, *sk next dc, [1 tr into next tr, ch 2] 4 times, 1 tr into next tr; rep from * to last dc, sk last dc, [1 tr into next tr, ch 2] twice, 1 tr into

3rd of ch 4, turn.

ROW 5: Ch 3, 2 tr into next ch-2 sp, 1 tr into next tr, 2 tr into next ch-2 sp, sk next tr, 1 tr into next tr, * [2 tr into next ch-2 sp, 1 tr into next tr] 3 times, 2 tr into next ch-2 sp, sk next tr, 1 tr into next tr; rep from * to last ch-2 sp, 2 tr into last ch-2 sp, 1 tr into next tr, 2 tr into sp formed by ch-5, sk first 2 chs of ch-5, 1 tr into 3rd of ch-5, turn.

ROW 6: Ch 3, 2 tr into first tr, ch 2, sk next 3 tr, 1 dc into next tr, ch 5, sk next 3 tr, 1 dc into next tr, ch 2, sk next 3 tr, *5 tr into next tr, ch 2, sk next 3 tr, 1 dc into next tr, ch 5, sk next 3 tr, 1 dc into next tr, ch 2, sk next 3 tr; rep from * ending with 3 tr into 3rd of ch-3, turn.

Rep Rows 3–6 for length required, ending with a Row 5.

3 MINI CHEVRONS

Work a multiple of 10 chains plus 3.

ROW 1: (RS) 1 tr into 4th ch from hook, 1 tr into each of next 4 chs, *sk next 2 chs, 1 tr into each of next 4 chs, ch 2, 1 tr into each of next 4 chs; rep from * to last 6 chs, sk next 2 chs, 1 tr into each of next 3 chs, 2 tr into last ch, turn.

ROW 2: Ch 3, 1 tr into first tr, 1 tr into each of next 3 tr, *sk next 2 tr, 1 tr into each of next 3 tr, [1 tr, ch 2, 1 tr] into next ch-2 sp, 1 tr into each of next 3 tr; rep from * to last 6 tr, sk next 2 tr, 1 tr into each of next 3 tr, 2 tr into 3rd of beg skipped ch-3, turn.

ROW 3: Ch 3, 1 tr into first tr, 1 tr into each of next 3 tr, *sk next 2 tr, 1 tr into each of next 3 tr, [1 tr, ch 2, 1 tr] into next ch-2 sp, 1 tr into each of next 3 tr; rep from * to last 6 tr, sk next 2 tr, 1 tr into each of next 3 tr, 2 tr into 3rd of ch-3, turn.

Rep Row 3 for length required.

cosy

hat with stripes

Simple, clean-cut stripes transform our basic hat into something special. The stripes are worked in four colours, arranged in a repeating sequence of cream, yellow, orange and brown. On Rounds 1 to 10, change the yarn colour on every round, then work Rounds 11 to 13 in orange, and finish by working Round 14 in brown.

FUN WITH STRIPES

Once you are familiar with basic crochet techniques and stitches, have fun experimenting with striped variations. Work one-row stripes in a repeating or random colour sequence (like the Cosy hat) or vary the depth of the stripes by working varying numbers of rows or rounds in each colour. Stripe colours can contrast strongly or the effect can be made more subtle by using a restricted palette of shades of one colour plus one or more co-ordinating colours. Double and treble crochet stitches all look good worked in stripes.

1

WORKING STRIPES

1 FELTED BAG WITH LOOP FASTENING

This small bag was also worked in the round using shades of pink tapestry wool highlighted with a single stripe of bright blue. The pretty fastening is made from a twisted strip of felted double crochet stitched to the back of the bag.

2 FELTED BAG WITH SHOULDER STRAP

Worked in a selection of bright, clashing colours, this small bag was worked in rounds of double crochet, rather than in rows. To begin working a bag in the round, make a foundation chain to the desired length and work around both sides of the chain, in the same way as the basic slippers on page 27.

3 FELTED BAG WITH HANDLES

Felting an accessory that has been worked in stripes changes its appearance because neighbouring yarn colours blend with each other to create a softer effect. Worked in double crochet, this variation of the bag with grab handles on page 62 was worked using oddments of tapestry wool and double knitting wool in a wide range of colours. Yarns were joined wherever a length was used up, rather than at the side edges.

2

3

amanda

plastic shoulder bag

Strips cut from plastic carrier bags make a good yarn with which to crochet because they create a strong, hard-wearing fabric. You can crochet the basic bag pattern on page 25 with plastic strips to make a very large tote. Alternatively, here's an adaptation with fewer stitches and rows, and a shoulder strap.

YOU WILL NEED

- 30–40 plastic carrier bags, depending on size
- 12mm (US size P) crochet hook
- Plastic garden twine
- Yarn needle large enough to accommodate thickness of twine

FINISHED SIZE

Bag measures 30cm (12in) deep and 30cm (12in) wide, not including handle.

TENSION

$3^1/_2$ stitches and $5^1/_2$ rows to 10cm (4in) measured over double crochet using 12mm (US size P) hook.

PREPARING THE YARN

Cut and join the strips as shown at right.

WORKING THE BAG

Ch 16.

Work 17 rows of double crochet until the front measures 30cm (12in), ending with a RS row.

Fasten off yarn.

Work back to match front.

WORKING THE SHOULDER STRAP

Ch 3.

Work even in double crochet until the strap measures approximately 81cm (32in), ending with a WS row.

Fasten off yarn.

FINISHING THE BAG

Place the front and back pieces together with right sides facing and stitch together using plastic twine, taking the needle between individual stitches rather than stitching through the strips. Stitch each end of the strap securely in place to the wrong side of the bag, overlapping the edges by about 2.5cm (1in). Turn the bag right side out.

MAKING THE YARN

1 Lay each bag flat and cut off handles and bottom seam using sharp pair of scissors.

2 Fold plastic in half so folded side edges of bag align. Fold in half again to make strip.

3 Starting at one end and cutting through all layers in strip, cut strip into sections about 2.5–4cm (1–1^1/$_2$in) wide. Open out sections to form rings.

4 To connect rings, loop one over and behind another ring and carefully pull to connect both rings.

5 Pull connected rings to form knot. Pull gently to avoid plastic tearing.

6 Repeat from Step 4, rolling plastic 'yarn' into several balls. When making bag, connect end of old ball to new one by looping it in same way as Step 4.

amy

mittens with contrast cuff

In this project, novelty yarn has been used to add interest and texture to plain mittens. Make short mittens without a cuff (see Fluffy, page 42), then trim the cuff edge with a band of double or treble crochet worked with two eyelash yarns held together.

WORKING WITH NOVELTY YARNS

Novelty yarns come in many textures and may be a solid colour or space-dyed in attractive colour combinations. They can be used in small amounts as decorative accents or to replace a smooth yarn when working a pattern, providing they work up to the same tension.

Many novelty yarns are made from a mixture of fibres and need special care when washing. (Check the ball or skein band for the fibre composition and care details.) These yarns are more difficult to work with than smooth yarns. Concentrate and count carefully when crocheting because it's harder to distinguish individual stitches than when working with smooth yarns.

WORKING WITH NOVELTY YARNS

The swatches below give you an idea of the different types of novelty yarns available. Each yarn is contrasted against a smooth chunky yarn made from pure wool.

1 MOHAIR YARN

Mohair yarns are soft and fluffy and contain a high proportion of kid mohair spun around a synthetic core for strength. If you find mohair yarn feels itchy next to the skin, use it in small amounts as a trim rather than to make the main part of an accessory.

2 RIBBON YARN

Ribbon yarns are woven in a flat strip and come in different widths and weights. The yarn in this swatch is made from cotton and nylon and changes colour at intervals, shading from blue to plum. The ribbon yarn is held together with a solid-coloured smooth yarn to add thickness.

3 TEXTURED YARN

Novelty yarns made from pure wool or wool/synthetic mixtures create a wide range of textures and colours. Yarns may be textured with loops, bobbles and slubs or be twisted to vary from very fine to very thick at regular intervals along the yarn. The yarn in the swatch is spun mainly from wool with smaller amounts of acrylic and nylon.

4 EFFECT YARN

Effect yarns, or component yarns, come in different fibre combinations and textures to add colour and sheen to your work without adding bulk. The swatch shows an effect yarn made from nylon held together with the main chunky yarn.

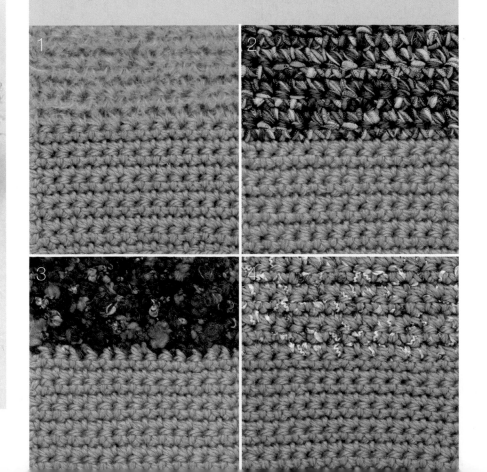

violet

felted bag

These two bags were made from the basic buttonhole bag pattern on page 25 using two strands of Shetland double knitting wool held together. The dark purple bag was machine washed in hot water, the light purple bag was not washed so is unfelted.

FELTING SWATCHES

Felting or—to give the process the correct term—fulling, describes deliberately shrinking a piece of crocheted fabric so that it thickens and becomes solid, yet still pliable. Double crochet gives the best results and the fabric shrinks fairly evenly lengthwise and widthwise. The amount of shrinkage will vary depending on how loosely the piece has been crocheted, the temperature and length of the wash, and the amount of friction.

The easiest way to felt something is to machine wash it, adding an old towel or pair of jeans to the machine for extra friction. Pull the wet fabric gently into shape and lay it flat to dry. This may take several days, depending on the weather and the thickness of the felt.

Pure wool yarns are used for felting, but avoid those that are treated to be machine washable, as most will not felt. The best types to try are wools labelled as 'hand wash only'. Some yarns lose stitch definition quickly when washed, while others may need several washes before you get the effect you want. Remember that felting is an inexact science so always crochet a swatch and wash and dry it first before starting to crochet your project. Keep on swatching until you're happy with the results.

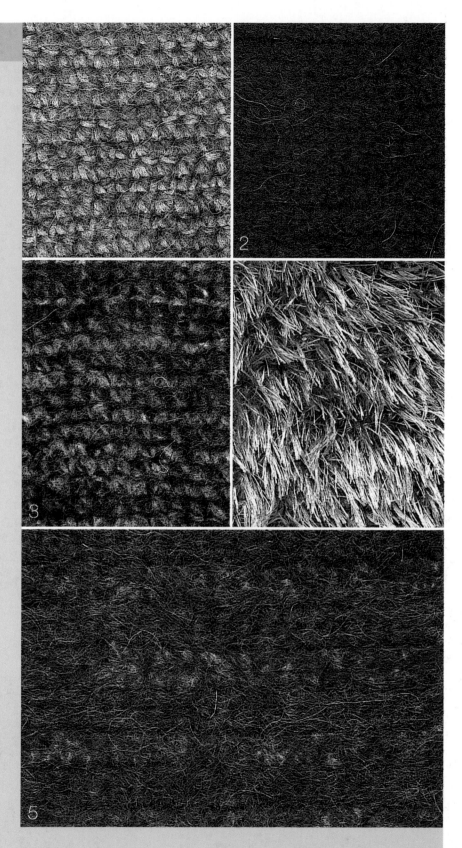

1 TWO STRANDS OF SHETLAND WOOL

Double crochet worked in two contrasting colours of Shetland double knitting wool held together. Washed in hot water, this type of wool felts really well, making a thick, even fabric that thickens up nicely.

2 CHUNKY WOOL

Double crochet worked in a pure wool chunky yarn and washed twice in hot water. After the first wash, the fabric was too thin and still showed a lot of stitch definition. After the second hot wash, the yarn had felted a little bit too much, resulting in a hard, rather stiff fabric.

3 ICELANDIC WOOL PLUS RIBBON YARN

Double crochet worked with one strand of light Icelandic wool and one strand of silk/viscose ribbon yarn and washed in hot water. This has a lovely soft finish; the stitch definition is still there but the fabric has thickened up nicely.

4 ICELANDIC WOOL PLUS EYELASH YARN

Double crochet worked with one strand of light Icelandic wool and one strand of synthetic eyelash yarn and washed in hot water. The wool component has felted and shrunk less than the other samples because the contrast yarn won't felt. The fabric is soft yet substantial with a lovely furry surface.

5 ICELANDIC WOOL PLUS MOHAIR

Two-row stripes worked in double crochet using one strand of Icelandic yarn and two strands of solid colour mohair yarn and washed in hot water. The felt feels thick and substantial, but is still very soft.

spice

slippers with surface crochet

Surface crochet is a technique that adds decoration to a previously worked crochet background. A round or row of surface crochet looks similar to embroidered chain stitch, but it's worked with a hook through the fabric. Decorate slippers, as shown here, or use rows of surface crochet to add colour to a plain buttonhole bag.

YOU WILL NEED

- 2 [2, 3] balls of pure wool chunky yarn with approx 92m (100yd) per 100g ball
- Oddments of the same weight yarn in 4 contrasting bright colours
- 5mm (US size H), 6mm (US size J), and 6.5mm (US size K) crochet hooks or sizes needed to achieve tension
- Yarn needle

FINISHED SIZES

To fit sizes Small (to fit up to 23cm/9in sole), Medium (to fit up to 25.5cm/10in sole) and Large (to fit up to 28cm/11in sole).

TENSION

14 stitches and 16 rows to 10cm (4in) measured over double crochet worked with 6mm (US size J) hook or size needed to achieve tension.

MAKING THE SLIPPERS

Crochet and finish the slippers following the basic slippers pattern on page 27.

WORKING THE DECORATION

1 Thread 1 of the contrasting yarns in yarn needle. Secure end of yarn on wrong side of slipper back by working 1 or 2 stitches into crochet.

2 Insert 5mm (US size H) hook through slipper just below row of slip stitch edging and close to where contrasting yarn is secured. Wrap yarn over hook and pull loop of yarn through to right side.

3 Holding contrast yarn on wrong side, insert hook into crochet 1 stitch below and pull another loop of yarn to right side, taking it through both crochet and loop already on hook to make slip stitch.

4 Continue in this way, working around slipper and making 1 slip stitch in each hole between slipper stitches until round is complete. Secure yarn on wrong side in same way as Step 1. Repeat with 3 remaining colours, spacing rounds 1 stitch apart.

chapter 6
gallery

The Gallery contains a photograph of **every accessory and variation** in the book. The projects are grouped so that accessories of the same type are shown together, making it easy to see the kinds of embellishments used. **Browse** through the pictures and enjoy working out what you'll choose to make for your next crochet project, but don't forget that there are many **more combinations** you can create using the techniques in the book. Try adding fluffy pompoms to a felted bag, stitch chunky beads or brightly coloured buttons onto a hat, or work bands of glittering sequins on a scarf – the **choice** is yours.

SCARVES

Copper, page 56

Scarf with ball buttons and loops

Erica, page 58

Scarf with strip closure

Susie, page 32

Narrow scarf with pom-poms

Priscilla, page 34

Scarf with shell edging

Jazz, page 36

Scarf with granny square

pockets

Elegant, page 78

Scarf with crocheted-in beads

Patience, page 106

Lacy shell scarf

SCARF VARIATIONS

Looped scarf, page 51

Scarf with looped edging

Pyramid, page 80

Scarf with beaded felt circles

Fringed scarf, page 41

Scarf with yarn fringe

Button scarf, page 87

Scarf with button trim

Paris, page 82

Scarf with beaded fringe

Frilled scarf, page 45

Scarf with frill

Curly scarf, page 95

Scarf with curlicue fringe

BAGS

Summer, page 38

Bag with crochet flower trim

Arizona, page 40

Bag with yarn fringe

Lauren, page 64 (right)

Clutch bag with triangular flap

Orient, page 60

Bag with bamboo handles

Hearts, page 62

Bag with grab handles

Snowflake, page 84

Felted bag with sequins

Nordic, page 86

Felted bag decorated with buttons

Glitter, page 100

Small evening bag

Sarah, page 104

Mesh tote bag

BAG VARIATIONS

Pocket bag, page 37

Bag with granny square pocket

Button and loop bag, page 56

Bag with ball buttons and loops

Amanda, page 110

Plastic shoulder bag

Glamorous bag, page 43

Bag with marabou trim

Shallow bag, page 61

Bag with painted wooden handles

Violet, page 114

Felted bag

Felt-trimmed bag, page 53

Bag with pinked felt strips

Shoulder bag, page 63

Bag with shoulder strap

Toggle bag, page 67

Bag with toggle fastening

Tab bag, page 75

Bag with hook-and-loop
fastening

**Felted bag with handles,
page 109**

Punk bag, page 69

Bag with decorative zippers

Glitzy bag, page 83

Bag with beaded fringe

**Felted bag with shoulder
strap, page 109**

Braided bag, page 71

Bag with braided fastening

Hearts and stars, page 89

Bag decorated with jewels

**Felted bag with loop
fastening, page 109**

HATS

College, page 46

Hat with crab stitch edging

Anna, page 70

Hat with crochet braids

Flapper, page 72 (below)

Hat with earflaps

Molly, page 92

Hat with ring buttons

Curly, page 94

Hat with curlicues

Topknot, page 48

Hat with crochet tassel

Loopy, page 50

Hat with looped edging

Happy, page 102

Stocking hat with pompoms

MITTENS

Fluffy, page 42

Shortie mittens with marabou trim

Snappy, page 68

Shortie mittens with decorative zipper

Cozy, page 108

Hat with stripes

Florence, page 44

Mittens with frilled cuff

Jewel, page 88

Mittens with jewel trim

Liberty, page 90

Mittens with shells and bells

HAT VARIATIONS

Appliqué hat, page 81

Hat with beaded felt circles

Toggle, page 66

Mittens with toggle fastening

Amy, page 112

Mittens with contrast cuffs

SLIPPERS

Zigzag, page 52

Slippers with felt trim

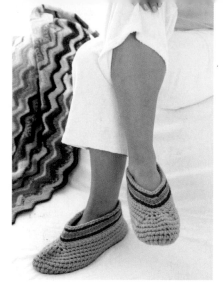

Spice, page 116

Slippers with surface crochet

MITTEN VARIATIONS

Glitzy mittens, page 85

Mittens with sequin decoration

Sporty, page 74

Slippers with tab fastening

SLIPPER VARIATIONS

Shell-edged slippers, page 35

Slippers with shell edging

Ring mittens, page 93

Mittens with ring buttons

Charming, page 96

Slippers with novelty charms

Edged slippers, page 47

Slippers with crab stitch edging

Index

Acknowledgments

Breslich & Foss Ltd and Jan Eaton would like to thank the following individuals for their help in the creation of this book: Alicia Ryan and Tashi Archdale for modelling the accessories; Jackie Jones for styling the hair and make-up; Martin Norris for all the photography; Hazel Williams for checking the patterns and Marie Clayton for editorial assistance. Last but not least, our thanks go to designer Elizabeth Healey, whose original concept this series was.